The Observer's Pocket Series

TREES

The Observer Books

A POCKET REFERENCE SERIES COVERING A
WIDE RANGE OF SUBJECTS

Natural History

BIRDS
BIRDS' EGGS
BUTTERFLIES
LARGER MOTHS
COMMON INSECTS
WILD ANIMALS
ZOO ANIMALS
WILD FLOWERS
GARDEN FLOWERS
FLOWERING TREES
    AND SHRUBS
CACTI
TREES
GRASSES
HOUSE PLANTS
COMMON FUNGI
LICHENS
POND LIFE
FRESHWATER FISHES
SEA FISHES
SEA AND SEASHORE
GEOLOGY
ASTRONOMY
WEATHER
CATS
DOGS
HORSES AND PONIES

Transport

AIRCRAFT
AUTOMOBILES
COMMERCIAL VEHICLES
SHIPS
MANNED SPACEFLIGHT
UNMANNED SPACEFLIGHT
BRITISH STEAM
    LOCOMOTIVES

The Arts etc

ARCHITECTURE
CATHEDRALS
CHURCHES
HERALDRY
FLAGS
PAINTING
MODERN ART
SCULPTURE
FURNITURE
POTTERY AND
    PORCELAIN
MUSIC
POSTAGE STAMPS
BRITISH AWARDS AND
    MEDALS

Sport

ASSOCIATION FOOTBALL
CRICKET

Cities

LONDON

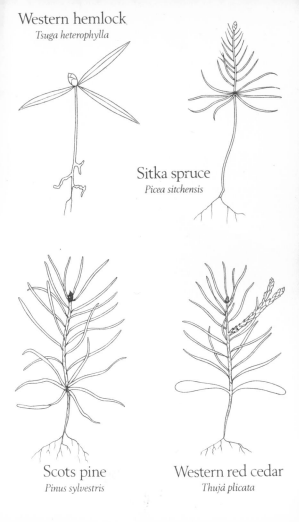

Western hemlock
Tsuga heterophylla

Sitka spruce
Picea sitchensis

Scots pine
Pinus sylvestris

Western red cedar
Thuja plicata

The Observer's Book of

TREES

COMPILED BY
HERBERT L. EDLIN
B.Sc., Diploma in Forestry, F.Inst.For.

DESCRIBING 74 SPECIES
WITH 51 COLOUR ILLUSTRATIONS
AND 58 HALF-TONE PHOTOGRAPHS

FREDERICK WARNE & CO LTD

FREDERICK WARNE & CO INC

LONDON : NEW YORK

For Camilla

ISBN 0 7232 1532 4

Printed in Great Britain by
Butler & Tanner Limited
Frome and London

74.10

CONTENTS

ACKNOWLEDGEMENTS

The colour illustrations and black and white outlines of fully grown trees are by Ian Garrard. The photographs of boles and bark are mainly by Maurice Nimmo; others are by the author. Line drawings showing twigs and buds of broadleaved trees and the key drawings of conifers are based on Forestry Commission material. Herbert Edlin drew the tree seedlings for the endpapers and took the photograph appearing on page 18.

The author and publishers wish to thank the following for their kind permission to reproduce photographs: the Forestry Commission (pages 13 and 15); Dartington Woodlands Ltd (page 17); British Leyland Ltd (page 21); Robert M. Adam (page 23); and J. H. Johns (page 24).

PUBLISHER'S NOTE

Wayside and Woodland Trees, also written by Herbert L. Edlin and published by Frederick Warne & Co. Ltd, gives a fuller account of this subject, with descriptions of additional trees and a further range of pictures.

The colour illustrations in this present book are also available in the form of four wall charts, published by Frederick Warne & Co. Ltd.

The first edition of *The Observer's Book of Trees*, compiled by W. J. Stokoe, appeared in 1937. Text and illustrations have been completely reshaped for this new 1975 edition.

PREFACE

The study of trees can provide interest and enjoyment at every season of the year, especially when the observer has the knowledge to identify and appreciate each species. One of the main features of this small book is therefore its coloured illustrations. These show each tree in the full glory of its summer foliage, flanked – in the case of those that lose their leaves in winter – by the characteristic outline of its bare winter branches. The distinctive winter buds that enable botanists to name any broadleaved tree in its leafless winter state are also shown in detail. A selection of photos of boles and bark, easily seen all round the year, will prove an invaluable guide to the naming of full-sized specimens. Seedling trees, in their first year of life, often look very unlike their parents, so two groups of line drawings, on the book's endpapers, are included to give adequate clues. Other sketches show key features of flowers, fruits and seeds, peculiar to each kind. It should be noted that these characters, though extremely useful, are only available for a few weeks each year, and then only on mature trees.

The text describes the seasonal changes in the appearance of every tree which affect the evergreens as well as the deciduous broadleaved kinds. A tree is a living organism that reflects the rising warmth of spring by putting forth fresh shoots and leaves, followed, or sometimes preceded, by flowers that ripen into fruits with characteristic seeds. In autumn it foreshadows the coming cold of winter by slowing down its growth and, in many kinds, losing its foliage, which assumes marvellous autumn tints before falling. You must take your tree as you find it. To the keen observer in the active seasons it will seldom be the same two weeks, or even two days, together.

Trees have also their longer, overall life pattern, from seedling through sapling and then robust middle age, when they blossom and bear seeds, to their eventual fall before the woodsman's axe, or before a great gale after decay has sapped their inner strength. Be ready, then, to fit each tree into its age group. Consider, too, whether it first arose naturally from a self-sown seed, or was planted. In the latter event, try to discover why. Did a landscape gardener place it where it stands for ornament, or is it one of a crop set out by an industrious forester to yield timber?

Nowadays around 40,000 hectares (100,000 acres) of land are afforested or re-afforested in Britain every year, while widespread planting of specimen trees for shelter or scenery takes place in parks, streets and gardens everywhere. Trees preferred for both purposes, some native, but many introduced from abroad, will be found described in these pages, which hold an account of the eighty-two kinds you are most likely to encounter.

CLASSIFIED INDEX
Families, Genera and Species

The abbreviation 'L.' stands for Linnaeus, the great Swedish botanist.

9

INTRODUCTION

The Tree and the Forest

How Trees Live and Grow

Trees are land plants with woody stems that have the power to grow steadily larger over long spans of years. They are distinguished from shrubs by their distinct main trunks, which develop because one of the tallest shoots gains dominance over its competitors, and is therefore called 'the leader'. This results in greater height growth than shrubs achieve, with a high spreading crown of foliage rather than a low bushy one.

Trees start life as seedlings, springing from small seeds, and may end it as centuries-old giants of the forest. In Britain outstanding individual trees can reach 55 m (181 ft) in height, with girths, conventionally measured at breast-height (1.3 m or 4 ft 3 in. from the ground), of 13.1 m (43 ft). In favourable regions of California related trees grow to twice those sizes; the record height today is held by a coast redwood, 117 m (384 ft) tall, and the tree of greatest girth is a giant sequoia 22.9 m (75 ft) round.

The secret of a tree's continued growth lies partly in the winter-resting buds at the tips of twigs, which enable the shoots to grow longer each year, and partly in a marvellous sheath of tissue called the *cambium*. This cambium, only one cell thick, surrounds every woody stem, and even extends to the underground roots. During the growing season, it adds a fresh layer of woody tissue to the stem it surrounds, by throwing off new cells on its inward side. Thus, each spring, the cambium adds a narrow zone of light, pale-coloured wood to the outside of the tree's woody core. This early *springwood* is followed

11

by a darker, denser and stronger zone of *summerwood*, and the two together form one *annual ring*. In this way all tree stems get stouter as they grow older, and the base of each tree trunk expands to match the growing weight of the crown of branches and foliage above.

There are no fixed limits to the size or life-span of a tree. Ages exceeding 100 years are frequent, and can easily be proved by counting the annual rings on the base of a felled tree — or its stump. Oaks occasionally attain 500 years, exceptional yews 1000, Californian redwoods 3000, and bristle cone pines in the Arizona deserts as much as 4000 years.

Unless a tree is felled for timber, its life is usually ended through internal decay, caused by a fungus that gains entry through some chance branch wound, and slowly spreads through the wood of its trunk. Eventually the weakened stem collapses, and the whole tree slowly rots away on the forest floor.

Trees, like other plants, need a constant supply of water in order to live, and this is drawn in from the soil by a huge network of long, though shallow, roots. This water flows up the woody zone of each stem, as *root sap*, carrying with it, in a very dilute solution, the mineral salts from the soil that are essential to all plant life. In a large stem, only the outer annual rings, called the *sapwood*, carry this flow. The inner rings, now called the *heartwood*, have undergone chemical changes and become darker, stronger and usually more durable. They no longer transport water actively but still serve to support the growing weight of the tree's crown, and to resist the force of strong winds.

When the root sap reaches the leaves it plays its part in the vital biochemical process called *carbon fixation*. The air that flows into the leaves holds a minute proportion, only about 0.03 per cent, of carbon dioxide gas. In the presence of sunlight, which provides essential energy, some of this gas combines with water to form carbohydrates. This process, called *photosynthesis*, can only occur with the aid of the marvellous chemical substance called *chlorophyll*, which is present in all the green parts of the tree or plant, but not elsewhere.

The carbohydrates so formed are carried away from the leaves, as a sugar solution, in a stream of leaf sap. This flows, mainly downwards, through the veins and stalks of the leaves and then through a special conductive tissue called the *bast*. The bast layer lies just below the bark, but outside the cambium. As each stem gets larger, the cambium adds fresh bast cells on its own outer surface. Through the bast and related conductive tissues every part of the tree, including its underground roots, receives the carbohydrate foodstuffs that it needs. Carbohydrates have two functions. They build up the tree's substance,

Sowing acorns to raise seedling oaks.

for all tree tissues, including wood, are composed of carbon compounds. They also provide fuel for all the tree's life processes. A small proportion of them is used up, by combining with the oxygen of the air, to release energy. This breathing process goes on in every part of the tree, both in sunlight and in the dark. It explains, for example, why seeds and roots can only grow in well-aerated soil.

Outside the bast lies a layer of bark, a corky waterproof material that protects all the living cells beneath it from drying out. It also gives protection from casual injury and from invasion by insects or harmful fungi. At first this bark is thin and smooth, but as the stems grow stouter a layer of cells beneath it, called the *bark cambium*, adds more and more layers of cork. As the bark gets thicker it splits up, or flakes off, in various ways peculiar to each kind of tree. This makes bark a very good aid to identification, especially as it is available low down and all the year round.

Most trees have distinctive leaf shapes, and these are illustrated in this book in the smaller drawings that accompany the whole-tree pictures. But most of our commoner trees are deciduous ones, which lose their leaves in autumn. Few people realize how easy it is to name most of these, all the winter through, by the placement and shape of the resting buds on every twig.

Every tree, whether broadleaved or coniferous, has its own particular habit of growth, which is the outcome of the basic bud plan on its small shoots. This is illustrated in the main colour painting of each tree. Where appropriate the leafless winter outline is also shown. These characteristic shapes only reach full development where the tree is 'open-grown', that is, standing in a broad park or hedgerow where it can spread naturally. Within a plantation, where the shape of each tree's crown is influenced by its neighbours close at hand, they are inevitably less distinct, as well as being harder to see.

14

Weeding sapling rowan trees in a Forestry Commission nursery.

Trees do not bear flowers during their first few years of life as seedlings and saplings, and many kinds postpone flowering until they are over twenty years old and possibly 12 m (40 ft) high. For this reason, and also because they are available for only a short season of each year, the flowers of trees, though very distinctive, are of limited use for identification. On some trees, such as wild cherry and laburnum, the flowers follow the familiar pattern of common garden plants. Such flowers have green sepals for protection, gay petals to attract pollinating insects, nectaries to reward them, male stamens to shed golden pollen, and a female pistil to receive pollen carried by insects, usually from another tree. Many trees, however, are wind pollinated, and these typically bear catkins of

Felling a Sitka spruce with a power saw.

discourage some plants, birds and beasts, but encourage others, while the steady annual fall of leaf litter enriches the soil, restoring nutrients removed by the tree's roots.

The forest history of Europe, Asia and North America begins with the last great ice sheet of the Ice Age, which dwindled towards the North Pole about 15,000 years ago. As the ice retreated and the soil warmed up, the low plants of the tundra slowly moved northwards, followed by the hardiest trees. Birches, spruces, pines and alders, trees that we still find farthest north or highest on the mountains, spread from the warmer regions farther south, where they had survived the Ice Ages. They were followed by the broadleaved trees that need more summer heat for vigorous growth and the ripening of their larger seeds, such as oak, beech and ash. Along with the trees came their related wild life, first the reindeer of the tundra, then red deer, elk or moose, bear, bison, wild cattle, wolf and lynx. The history of this natural forest's spread can be traced by the pollen grains of the various trees, which remain preserved in deep peat beds, just as the fossil bones of wild beasts of the past enable us to reconstruct the animal life in certain areas.

At first the only men to live in these wild forests were the hunters and fishermen of the Old Stone Age, who have recorded their presence by the flints they chipped to make tools and weapons. But gradually, around 2500 B.C., men of the Neolithic or New Stone Age began to migrate north. These people were herdsmen and cultivators as well as hunters, but had only stone tools. Slowly they made small clearings in the woods, on which to cultivate grain. After they had felled the trees, they burnt the branchwood to increase the fertility of the soil, and when one patch of land was exhausted, they moved on and cleared another. Their small flocks of sheep, herds of cattle and horses grazed on the former grain fields and checked the return of the trees. Gradually the once unbroken forest gave way, here and there, to fields

19

of grain, pastures and meadows for hay, adjoining the scattered homesteads.

Forest clearances were intensified in the Old World when the Bronze Age men, who arrived about 2000 B.C., began to use bronze axes. Later, about 500 B.C., other immigrants from southern Europe brought the knowledge of how to work iron, a stronger and more plentiful metal, which we still use, in the form of steel, for saws and axes today. Man's mastery of the virgin forest was now complete, and the farmers' clearings spread until eventually all the better land was used for crops or livestock. Poorer land, especially on steep and rocky mountainsides, remained under forest. The proportion over most of Europe, Asia and America today is about 25 per cent. But Britain has only 8 per cent of its area under trees, and most of this is not natural, but the outcome of recent artificial planting.

During the 17th century landowners began to realize that forest clearance had been taken too far in the British Isles. The needs of the relatively small rural population for fencing, building timbers, fire-wood, tanbark and charcoal wood for smelting iron were still being met from native woods. But this was only possible because the trees concerned, especially oak and hazel, grew again from sprouts, in woods managed as *coppices*, every time these were cut over. Supplies of larger timber, needed above all for building warships, were dwindling. John Evelyn, famous as a diarist and statesman during the Restoration period, published in 1664 his famous book: *Sylva, or a Discourse of Forest Trees, and the Propagation of Timber in His Majesty's Dominions* to encourage the rebuilding of the nation's woodland resources.

Landowners responded readily to this patriotic appeal, and for the next 250 years they planted trees on an impressive scale. Around their mansion houses they laid out broad parks and filled these and their landscape gardens with fine specimen trees. When they enclosed the old

20

open fields with hedgerows they planted oak, elm, and ash at intervals, partly for shelter, partly as a future source of timber. On their poorer lands, unsuited to agriculture, they made plantations of oak, beech, ash and sycamore, as leading broadleaved trees, or pine, spruce and larch as their principal conifers. Most of the mature trees one sees today, planted before 1920, are the result of this sustained effort in landscape planning which was aimed at the best possible use of each proprietor's land. Trees provided shelter for farm fields, cover for game, and magnificent scenery, as well as becoming a valuable and renewable resource as timber producers.

The Industrial Revolution of the 19th century, however, soon intensified the national demand for timber to a level that the home woods could no longer supply. By 1914, when the First World War began, nine-tenths of the wood used for building, packaging, mine supports and the transport industry, together with paper made from

Loading a spruce log for the sawmill, in Thornthwaite Forest, Cumbria.

wood pulp, was being imported from abroad. The shortages due to this war led the Government, in 1919, to set up a Forestry Commission, financed by the Treasury. Since then, this Commission has promoted research, has encouraged landowners to replant and expand their woodlands, and has planted over 800,000 hectares (2,000,000 acres) of forests on its own estates. To match the needs of industry, most of the trees planted have been the conifers which yield softwoods. To suit the land available, mostly in the northern and western uplands, new trees have been brought in. These include Sitka spruce, lodgepole pine, Douglas fir and western hemlock, all native to the west coast of North America. At many of the Commission's 226 forests, remarkably well spread over every county of England, Scotland and Wales, provision is now being made for the public to explore forest trails from car parks with picnic sites. Landscape values, and the conservation of wild life, soil and water resources are all carefully considered when new plantations are laid out. The Commission is now, in the 1970s, planting 16,000 hectares (40,000 acres) of new forests each year, while private landowners are adding a further 24,000 hectares (60,000 acres). Similar afforestation activities are going ahead in all parts of Ireland too.

At the same time, there has been a revival of interest in establishing trees for scenery and shelter, rather than as sources of timber, as shown by the national 'Plant a Tree Year' in 1973. This activity is widely based, bringing into its sphere suburban gardeners, farmers, managers of public parks, developers of housing estates, and highway authorities, as well as nurserymen and foresters. It has come at an opportune moment, because time was fast taking its toll of the heritage of tall trees established by earlier landowners. In the foreseeable future, there will be more trees and a greater variety of species for the countrygoer to observe than ever before.

*Coniferous woodland: native Scots pines in Glen Affric
Forest, Inverness-shire, Scottish Highlands.*

Broadleaved woodland: beech and oak in Park Hill Wood, Forest of Dean, Gloucestershire.

NAMING BROADLEAVED TREES

All our common broadleaved trees are distinguished from the conifers, or needle-leaved trees, by the broad blade, or broad separate leaflets, of each leaf. They are also called 'hardwoods', because the wood of most, though not all, is harder than the softwoods of the conifers. Another common name is 'deciduous trees' because, in contrast to most conifers, which are 'evergreens', their leaves fall in autumn and new foliage appears next spring. The few evergreen broadleaves, such as holly and holm oak, are easily known by their thick, glossy, dark-green leaves adapted to resist water loss in cold weather.

Evergreen trees can be identified by their leaves the whole year round, but most broadleaved trees stand leafless for five months, from mid-November to mid-April. The key to identification in winter, and indeed at most times of the year, is their bud pattern. For this reason, four pages of this book are devoted to the illustration of characteristic winter buds, with notes on their features. From midsummer on, the bud pattern can be determined by stripping a few leaves from a twig, for next winter's buds are formed well before autumn. The first point to note is whether the buds are borne alternately, that is, singly at intervals along the twigs (as in beech), or else in opposite pairs (*see* ash).

Leaves, available through spring, summer and early autumn, fall into three groups. They may be simple, unlobed leaves, with the outline of a common geometric figure, such as an oval (hornbeam), a conventional heart (lime) or a modified triangle (birch). Or they may be lobed, that is, partly divided into projecting sections, either *palmately* – spreading like the fingers of a hand (field maple) – or *pinnately* like a feather (oak). The third group of leaves are compound ones, having several leaflets isolated from each other, though springing from a common leaf-stalk. These, too, may be spread out *palmately* or fanwise (as in horse chestnut) or *pinnately* along the stalk (walnut). Leaves are shown in small sketches beside the whole-tree pictures.

Features constant the whole year round are the bark and the general habit of the tree. Though it becomes easy, with practice, to name a tree on sight by one of these characters, they are not nearly so easy to describe in words. Here the whole-tree illustrations and photos of bark and bole, which accompany most tree descriptions, will be your best guide.

Botanists classify trees by their flower-structure, but flowers are only available for a few weeks each year, and then only on large, well-established trees. Foresters, gardeners, and observers generally must be able to name any tree at sight, when no flowers can be found, or even when the tree is still a young sapling. If, however, a tree is found at flowering time, its flower characters will readily confirm an identification made by other means.

Those trees (like cherry) that bear showy insect-pollinated flowers, with large petals, are the easiest to recognize. Many other broadleaved trees (such as alder) bear quaint catkins, usually with male flowers in one structure and female flowers in a separate one, often very different in appearance. Some kinds of tree always bear male and female flowers on separate individual trees (poplars and willows for example).

In autumn come the fruits, holding seeds, and broadleaved trees have such a variety of both structures that identification becomes easy. Distinguish first between hard nuts (sweet chestnut), soft fruits holding stone-like seeds (hawthorn), and wind-borne seeds that may have tufts of hairs (plane) or broad-bladed wings (ash). Other trees bear small, simple seeds in pods (laburnum).

The seedlings of broadleaved trees always have *two* seed-leaves. These usually emerge from the seed-coat, but in some trees – the oak is one – they remain within it, serving as food-stores. The first 'juvenile' foliage is often unlike that of an adult tree. The characteristic appearance of common tree seedlings is shown on the endpapers of this book.

Finally, if a cut section of a log is available, the colours and characters of its inner heartwood and sapwood may help you to identify it.

IDENTIFICATION BY TWIGS AND BUDS

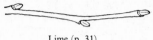

Lime (p. 31)

Twigs red, zigzag, smooth, shining; only 2 bud-scales seen, one larger than the other.

Spindle tree (p. 37)

Twigs sage green, becoming square as they expand.

Alder buckthorn (p. 41)

Buds opposite, with smooth scales. Twigs dark purplish brown.

Horse chestnut (p. 43)

Buds opposite, large, up to 2.5 cm (1 in.), dark brown, becoming sticky.

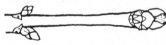

Sycamore (p. 46)

Buds opposite; yellowish-green scales with dark-brown markings.

Field maple (p. 49)

Buds opposite, scales hairy at tips, red-brown. Older twigs with corky ridges.

Laburnum (p. 52)

Twigs greyish green, ribbed. Exposed bud-scales about 4, with silvery-haired scales.

IDENTIFICATION BY

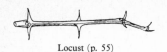

Locust (p. 55)

Paired spines beside alternate, minute buds on ribbed twigs. Bundle traces 3, leaf-scars membraneous.

Cherry (p. 58)

Buds alternate, large, glossy brown, ovoid, with about 6 exposed scales, grouped near twig tips.

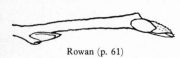

Rowan (p. 61)

Buds large, woolly, dark purple, appearing 'stalked' at base.

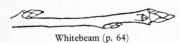

Whitebeam (p. 64)

Buds large, green, elongated, hairy at tips, on grey twigs.

Hawthorn (p. 67)

Twigs greyish, spiny; buds minute, rounded.

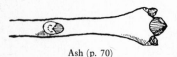

Ash (p. 70)

Buds paired, with black scales; terminal bud the largest, on flattened tip; twigs smooth, ash grey.

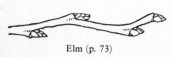

Elm (p. 73)

Buds alternate, blackish red, ovoid, bluntly tipped. Twigs zigzag.

TWIGS AND BUDS

Plane (p. 79)

Buds large, conical, enclosed by a single scale.

Walnut (p. 82)

Buds oval, blunt; vein traces on leaf-scars in 3 compound groups.

Birch (p. 85)

Twigs slender, flexible, often warty; buds minute with 2 or 3 visible scales.

Alder (p. 88)

Buds stalked, with waxy purplish bloom; twigs reddish brown.

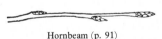

Hornbeam (p. 91)

Oval, alternate, many-scaled buds, bent inwards towards twigs.

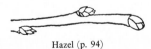

Hazel (p. 94)

Buds pale brown, blunt; twigs often clad in glandular bristles.

Pedunculate oak (p. 97)

Buds clustered at shoot tip, with numerous 5-ranked scales.

IDENTIFICATION BY TWIGS AND BUDS

Turkey oak (p. 103)

Buds clustered, surrounded by long narrow stipules.

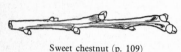

Sweet chestnut (p. 109)

Twigs reddish brown, longitudinally ridged towards projections bearing oval buds.

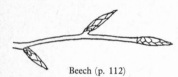

Beech (p. 112)

Twigs slender, buds spiky, spindle shaped, spreading, pale brown, 1.25 cm ($\frac{1}{2}$ in.) long.

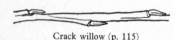

Crack willow (p. 115)

Buds appressed to twig. Only one visible bud-scale.

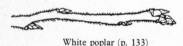

White poplar (p. 133)

Young twigs covered with white, cottony film.

Black poplar (p. 137)

Buds large, oval, chestnut brown, glossy, often resinous.

LIME

Tilia × vulgaris   TILIACEAE

The common lime, widely planted in parks and gardens, is a hybrid between two native species, which grow as rarities in a few ancient woodlands. One is the small-leaved lime, *Tilia cordata*, found in the Lake District and the Welsh Borders, which bears smaller leaves, about 5 cm

(2 in.) across. The other is the broadleaved lime, *T. platy-phyllos*, found in the eastern counties, which has larger leaves, up to 10 cm (4 in.) wide. Since the common lime rarely bears fertile seed, it is increased by cuttings or layering.

In winter all limes can be easily recognized by their curious buds set alternately along reddish, somewhat zigzag twigs. Every bud shows only two external scales, one being much larger than the other. The leaves, which open late in April, are shaped like the conventional heart in a pack of cards, but their bases are often uneven; they have long stalks, a toothed edge, and a pointed tip. They are pale green and tender when they open late in April, and may even be eaten as salads. Later they darken, and in autumn they turn gold before falling. Around mid-summer they are often attacked by tiny aphids which suck their sap and secrete sweet honeydew. Spots fall on pavements – or parked cars – below, and mould fungi turn the sticky deposit black.

Lime flowers open in May, in clusters at the end of a long stalk that bears a good key feature, an oblong leafy bract. Each flower has five sepals, five yellowish-white petals, and nectaries to attract bees; lime is a major honey-yielder. The fragrant flowers are sometimes picked and dried, then used to infuse lime-blossom tea; lime is related botanically to the tea bush. At the heart of each flower stand numerous golden stamens and a pistil. After pollination, the ovary ripens to a hard round box, holding a single seed. When the flower-group falls away, the leafy bract acts as a wing, aiding wind dispersal. Seedlings, which often arise from seeds of the wild species, have curious seed-leaves, divided like the fingers of a hand; normal foliage follows.

Lime wood has a pale, even, creamy-brown colour. It is soft, yet keeps a firm edge when carved, and works well in any direction. Wood carvers, such as the famous Grinling Gibbons, have always preferred it as the most apt medium for fine wood sculpture. It is also used for hat-blocks, shoe-lasts and, because it is very stable, for piano keys.

Limes are widely planted as park and avenue trees, because they have a pleasing outline and grow fast to great heights. A tree in Great Limes Wood, Duncombe Park, Yorkshire reaches 47 m (154 ft) and is Britain's tallest broadleaved tree; girths up to 6.4 m (21 ft) occur.

Lime bark is smooth and purplish grey. It is very fibrous within, and countrymen formerly used strips of lime bark peeled from logs, colloquially called 'bast', for tying bundles, or twisted them into ropes.

Smooth at first, lime later develops boldly ribbed grey bark and a buttressed base.

HOLLY

Ilex aquifolium   AQUIFOLIACEAE

Everyone knows holly at once by its tough, evergreen, glossy leaves, normally dark green above and pale green below. One must stress 'normally' because Victorian gardeners delighted in finding odd strains of holly with golden, silver, or variegated leaves, which they propagated by grafting on the common stock. Normally, too, the lower leaves of a holly tree are twisted; oval in shape, they bear sharp prickles at their angular twist-points, plus another point at the tip. Higher up, where there is no need for protection against browsing animals, there are no prickles, and each leaf is a simple pointed oval. Again, there are 'nurserymen's varieties' in which all the leaves are spineless or, alternatively, all prickly; one very spiky one is called 'hedgehog'.

Every flowering holly is either male or female. Whatever their sex, blossoms open in clusters in leaf axils in late May. Each flower has four green sepals, four white waxy petals, and either four stamens in the male, or a four-celled pistil in the female. They bear nectar and attract pollinating bees. By Christmas the ovaries of the female flowers ripen to the familiar red berries, each holding hard black seeds within the yellow pulpy flesh that attracts birds.

Seed, scattered on the ground, normally lies dormant through the next summer and winter before sprouting; nurserymen store berries carefully in damp sand for fifteen months. The first two seed-leaves are oval and soft, and fall after one summer; spiky evergreen foliage follows. Holly is one of several evergreen shrubs adapted to 'Mediterranean' climates of mild wet winters and hot dry summers. Its thick glossy leaves resist drought, yet remain active through cold winter months. This waxy foliage will burn fiercely, even on the living tree.

Holly bark is a smooth steel-grey shade, and remains smooth no matter how big the tree becomes. Very tall, slender hollies, up to 21 m (70 ft) are sometimes found in woodlands, and there are some fairly stout trees, up to 2 m (6 ft) round. The wood is an even, very pale brown, almost white colour, with no apparent difference between heartwood and sapwood. Being very dense, firm and stable, it is used for small turned or sculptured objects, such as bowls or chessmen, and in decorative inlaid work. If dyed black, it makes a fair substitute for ebony.

Holly bark is always smooth and grey; tree base may spread.

Remarkably, it holds so little water that it will burn when quite 'green', that is, freshly felled.

Holly makes an excellent hedge-shrub, for it stands clipping well and its spines stop animals forcing their way through. It gives year-round shelter against wind and noise, and forms a dense barrier that guarantees privacy.

SPINDLE

Euonymus europaeus   CELASTRACEAE

The spindle tree, as it is usually called, draws its name
from the age-long use of its thin stems as spindles for the
hand-spinning of wool. Before the spinning-wheel had
been invented, all the woollen thread needed for cloth
was spun by hand, usually by womenfolk (known as
spinsters) who twirled short sticks in one hand. One end
of the stick carried a thick hollow disc of stone or metal –
the spindle-whorl, which maintained a steady momentum.
With the other hand the spinner fed in loosely twisted
wool from a hank, and the spindle drew it out into tight
thread. Spindle trees provided the smoothest wood,
kindest to the fingers. Spindle-whorls, surviving for
centuries, give definite proof of human occupation on
prehistoric sites.

This pretty tree may be found scattered along hedgerows, on lime-rich soils, and particularly on chalk downs,
anywhere south of the Scottish Lowlands. It is easily
known because its younger twigs are dark green and
square, with four distinct angles; older stems become
round, with pale grey-brown bark. The smooth wood
below is greenish white. The leaves, set alternately, are
short-stalked, small and oval, with toothed edges. They
fade to beautiful orange-purple tints in October.

Spindle bears small, yellowish-green flowers on short
stalks in leaf axils in May. Conventional accounts state
that each tree is male or female, but individuals often
carry flowers holding both fertile stamens and a fertile
pistil. Each flower has four green sepals, four yellowish-
green petals, four stamens, and/or a central pistil with
a four-celled ovary. The fruit, green at first, turns bright
pink in autumn, and expands. The joints between its four
lobes then split, to reveal four seeds, each clad in bright
orange pulp. This lively colour contrast soon attracts the

birds that scatter the seeds, and people often gather spindle fruits for decoration. Gardeners, however, usually cultivate the south European broadleaved spindle, *Euonymus latifolius*, which grows faster on a wider range of soils, and bears bigger and brighter berries.

The hard black seeds within the orange pulp lie dormant on the ground through the winter and then sprout, bearing two oval seed-leaves.

Curious facts and even folk-lore are connected with the spindle tree. Its orange pulp yields a yellow dye, and its pink husk a red one, though it is a tedious job to harvest

Spindle's smooth grey bark eventually develops pink-tinged fissures.

them. The pulp, again, is a powerful purgative. The fruits as a whole are poisonous to people and sheep, though not to birds. Stewed, they give a shining hair rinse, but if kept dry and powdered they kill lice.

Purplish zones gradually form a network on alder buckthorn's smooth grey bark.

ALDER BUCKTHORN

Frangula alnus   RHAMNACEAE

This is a tree to look for on swampy ground in the Midlands and south of England; its odd name arises in part because it grows where alders do. The 'buckthorn' comes from its botanical relationship to the purging buckthorn *Rhamnus cathartica*, a spiny shrub bearing black berries, which grows on dry chalk downs. But alder buckthorn has no thorns at all!

Alder buckthorn has smooth, purplish-black bark with pale-brown breathing pores. The slender twigs carry oval leaves in rather irregular opposite pairs. These are dull green in summer, but change to vivid yellow before falling in autumn. The flowers are small greenish-yellow structures, carried on short stalks in groups in leaf axils. Each has five sepals, five stamens, and a central pistil. They yield nectar and are pollinated by insects when they open in May. The berries ripen through green and red to black juicy globes. In winter the birds strip them from the tree, helping to spread the hard black seeds within. These seeds lie dormant on the marshland soil for about eighteen months before they sprout. The seed-leaves remain in the seed.

Alder buckthorn never becomes a large tree. The maximum height is only 6 m (20 ft) and the greatest girth only 1 m (3 ft). Yet its timber, which has a rich brown heartwood within a paler sapwood zone, is harvested to obtain a remarkable charcoal. When this is mixed with sulphur and saltpetre, it makes a high-grade gunpowder that is still used in slow fuses to fire explosive charges. The even structure of alder buckthorn wood, and the resulting charcoal, ensure that every fuse burns reliably at a calculated rate.

Fortunately alder buckthorn readily resumes growth from its stumps after being cut back, so it is unlikely to

disappear from our wooded marshes. Its bark holds a powerful purgative, similar to cascara derived from a related Californian tree, *Rhamnus purshiana*. Alder buckthorn leaves are the preferred food of caterpillars of the lovely bright-yellow brimstone butterfly, and for this reason alone this charming small tree merits preservation in nature reserves.

HORSE CHESTNUT

Aesculus hippocastanum   HIPPOCASTANACEAE

Everybody recognizes this tree by its swollen brown buds, set in opposite pairs except for those at twig tips. People pick twigs in March, when the buds become sticky with gum, which is probably a protection against insect attack. They put them in jars of water to watch the leaves unfold in a coating of pale-brown downy hairs, a device to resist

water loss. These leaves, fully open by late April, have a peculiar 'palmately compound' pattern, with five or seven leaflets springing from one central stalk. Each leaflet broadens from its base, then tapers abruptly to a blunt tip; it is strongly veined, with a doubly toothed edge. Pale green at first, the leaves darken later and turn to gold before falling, in small fragments, in autumn, though some turn rust-red earlier.

Horse chestnut flowers open late in May in upright spikes, sometimes called 'candles', carried clear of the foliage. Each main stalk carries about fifteen separate short-stalked blossoms. Each of these has five green sepals, and a corolla of four or five showy white petals marked with reddish-brown 'honey guide' spots to direct visiting insects. The corolla is markedly uneven, or zygomorphic, the base being larger than the top. Five stamens, tipped with golden anthers, follow this curve, and so does the central style bearing the pollen-receiving stigma. A bee seeking nectar at the flower's heart is obliged to brush past both anthers and stigma, carrying pollen on its way.

The well-known horse chestnut seed, or 'conker', ripens by October within a thick, leathery, green husk, bearing brown spines; this husk usually splits when the fruit falls and hits the ground. Each glossy, hard, dark-brown seed has a paler patch, which has earned the tree its American name of 'buckeye'. If left on the ground, the chestnut sprouts next spring as a sturdy seedling which keeps its seed-leaves within the husk, and bears typical compound leaves from the outset. Many nuts are gathered by children for the game of conkers, originally 'conquerors'. They bore a hole in each nut and run a knotted string through. Then each player bashes his nut against that of his opponent, till one cracks and the harder nut wins.

Horse chestnut bark is purplish brown in colour and develops flat plates that scale off as the trunk ages. Trees grow moderately tall, up to 41 m (134 ft) with girths of

Horse chestnut's brown bark has oblong flakes; spiral buttresses are characteristic.

6.7 (22 ft). The wood is pale cream in colour, with no clear distinction of heartwood. It is relatively soft and non-durable, though easily worked, and is only used for small objects like trays, bowls or toys. Horse chestnut is planted only as an ornamental tree, to make a brave display in a park, along an avenue, or on some woodland fringe.

Introduced to Vienna from Istanbul in 1576, horse chestnut is so called because the Turks fed its nuts to broken-winded horses. But most animals, except deer, refuse to eat the tough bitter seeds that are so unlike the delicious sweet chestnuts.

45

SYCAMORE

Acer pseudoplatanus   ACERACEAE

The sycamore or great maple, a typical member of the maple or *Acer* genus, owes its common name to confusion with the *sycomorus*, or fig-mulberry, a bush with the same shape of leaf, mentioned in the Bible. In Scotland it is often called 'plane', because it resembles the true plane (*see* page 79), but the sycamore's leaves and buds are set *in opposite pairs*.

Sycamore was introduced from France in the Middle Ages, certainly by the 15th century. It has now become established throughout the British Isles, and regenerates everywhere from self-sown seed, just like a native tree. Very hardy, it has often been planted as shelter-belts or to protect hillside farmsteads, especially in the north of England. On fertile ground it soon becomes a tall timber tree, reaching 38 m (124 ft), with girths up to 6.7 m (22 ft).

Sycamore grows a smooth, purplish-grey bark, which develops shallow round plates that may flake away, leaving pinkish-brown patches beneath. Winter buds, set in pairs, are hard, tight, and green. The leaves, opening in April, are paired, with long reddish stalks, and have a characteristic lobed outline, with five rounded projections, and bays between. Dark green above, they are paler beneath. After changing through yellow to brown, they fall in October.

Flowers, opening in May, hang in long yellowish-green clusters from outer branches. The upper and lower flowers in each cluster are usually imperfect. Those half-way down have each a slender stalk, five green sepals, five yellow petals, five male stamens, and a central ovary, with two styles. After pollination by bees, this ovary ripens two paired seeds, each with a broad-bladed wing. Reddish green at first, the seeds and wings turn brown before

falling in October. Then they twirl round on the wind like the blades of a helicopter. Tucked away inside each seed is a seedling, with two long, strap-shaped seed-leaves that are already bright green – an unusual feature. Next spring the seeds sprout on the damp earth of the woodland floor, in garden beds, or even in gutters. Their seed-leaves are followed by oval primary leaves, then normal lobed ones.

Sycamore timber is pale creamy-brown in colour, very

hard, firm, and smooth when finished. Its special uses include furniture, flooring for dance-halls, turned bowls and ornaments and wooden rollers. It is the wood always used for the back, sides and stocks of all string instruments, such as violins and guitars, though the belly must be spruce.

Old sycamores develop oblong grey-brown bark flakes, and a buttressed base.

Finely divided, rough grey bark of field maple.

FIELD MAPLE

Acer campestre   ACERACEAE

The field maple is so called because it is usually found growing wild along hedgerows bordering fields, rather than as a cultivated tree. It is closely related to the syca-more, which is sometimes called the 'great maple'. Several clear points of difference appear. The twigs of field maple are slender and bear narrow, crimson-brown buds, not swollen ones as in sycamore. The bark is pale brown, rough and distinctly corky on the stouter twigs; it

develops fibrous plates on woody stems. The small leaves have deep rounded lobes and reddish stalks. In autumn they become a lovely bright golden shade.

Field maple blossoms open in May in short, hanging clusters. In each group the highest and lowest flowers are usually infertile. Fertile ones around the centre have five green sepals, five bright yellowish-green petals, eight stamens and a central pistil. Pollination is effected by insects. In October the fruits ripen as pairs of winged seeds, having a general resemblance to those of sycamore. Field maple fruits, however, are set directly opposite each other, and not at an angle, and their wings have a broader base and a marked reddish tinge. The seeds, spread by the wind, lie dormant in the soil for eighteen months before sprouting. Seedlings raise two seed-leaves, followed first by oval leaves and later by lobed ones.

Along the hedges field maple is usually lopped together with thorn bushes, so remains a stunted tree. Left to itself, it can reach 27 m (88 ft) tall, with a girth of 3.7 m (12 ft). Few trees become big enough for timber. A little maple wood is used for turnery or decorative wood-work. It is firm, smooth, and stable, and can be cut to exact forms with little risk of change of shape. In colour it is a warm pale brown, with slightly darker heartwood. The Welsh name of *masarn*, meaning maple, gave rise to the term 'mazer' for a small turned bowl of maple, often ornamented with silver.

Norway maple, *A. platanoides*, is a related but distinct tree, which grows larger than the field maple and is often planted for ornament. Its leaves are larger, paler green, and have distinctly pointed lobes. The seeds are bigger, too, with pale-brown wings set at a shallow angle to one another. Norway maple has a flowering pattern quite distinct from either field maple or sycamore. It opens *upright* clusters of bright greenish-gold flowers in late March, before its leaves have expanded, and is one of the gayest spectacles of spring. The autumn tints are a bright orange-brown. Native to Scandinavia and mid-European uplands, Norway maple has been grown here since about 1600.

LABURNUM

Laburnum anagyroides   PAPILIONACEAE

The lovely hanging blossoms of laburnum, which open
unfailingly every May, have ensured its widespread
planting in gardens everywhere. Each separate flower,
carried on its own short stalk from a long central one,
has the characteristic structure of the sweet pea family,
described for the locust tree (*see* page 56). Most laburnums
that people plant today are hybrids between varied
European and Asiatic species, selected for profusion of
flowers. They are propagated by grafting scions on stocks
of the common species. This, the Central European
laburnum, grows as a small wild tree in Switzerland and
neighbouring countries.

Laburnum is unusual in having trifoliate leaves, that
is, compound leaves, with only three leaflets. Each leaf is
carried on a short stalk, and the dark-green leaflets are
neat ovals. The winter buds, set alternately on greenish-
grey twigs, are pale grey and hairy. The bark on older
stems becomes a rich olive-green colour and remains
smooth.

After the short-lived laburnum flowers have faded, the
central green ovary enlarges and ripens to become a hard
black pod. Eventually this splits, twisting with a sudden
jerk, and the little hard black seeds within it are ejected
sharply, so aiding their dispersal. Children occasionally
nibble laburnum's hard black shiny seeds, which are
mildly poisonous, and fall ill as a result.

Laburnum never grows more than 10 m (32 ft) tall,
and the stoutest stems only reach 1 m (3 ft) in girth. Its
heartwood is a beautiful chocolate-brown colour, shot
through with lighter flecks; it is strong and naturally
durable. A thin zone of pale-yellow sapwood surrounds it.
The stems are never broad enough to provide constructional wood, but laburnum is widely used for decorative

purposes. It makes an attractive inlay for cabinet work, and if the stems are cut across obliquely, at an angle to the main axis, an exceptionally fine figure, called 'oyster-shell', results. Laburnum is also chosen for bowls and small pieces of wood sculpture.

Makers of 'wood-wind' musical instruments prefer laburnum because it is dense, stable, and has good resonance. It is used for flutes, oboes, and the chanters and drones of bagpipes.

Smooth green-grey laburnum bark.

Like all plants and trees of the sweet pea family, laburnum bears on its roots curious nodules, in which lives a bacterium, *Bacterium radicis*, which enables the plant to 'fix' the valuable nutrient nitrogen from the air. Hence these plants can flourish on poorer soils, and actually enrich, by the decay of their leaves, the ground where they grow.

LOCUST

Robinia pseudoacacia   PAPILIONACEAE

The strange name of this remarkable tree arises from
confusion with the locust bean tree of Israel, the fruits
of which enabled John the Baptist to survive in the
wilderness. It is also called 'false acacia' because it bears
spines but is not a real acacia, and 'Robinia' after Jean
Robin, the 17th-century French botanist who first described it. Native to eastern North America, it was discovered and named 'locust' by the first settlers. Promptly

introduced to Europe, it has been widely planted, usually as a decorative tree, but also to yield tough timber, poles and — on the Continent — fire-wood.

Locust can be told at once by the paired spines along its zigzag twigs. The winter buds, set alternately, are tiny and barely visible. Both branches and main stem continue the wayward course of the twigs, resulting in tortuous limbs with no long straight lengths. Last of our trees to leaf out, locust opens, in May, long compound leaves, each consisting of about a dozen round, smooth-edged leaflets, set along a long thin stalk, plus a solitary terminal leaflet. When the leaves eventually fall in October, they turn yellow and most leaflets break away from the main stalk.

Locust flowers open in June, in long hanging white chains which make a tall tree a gay display for a roadside or park. Each blossom on the chain resembles a sweet pea, for locust belongs to the same botanical family. It has five green sepals and five white petals fitted together in a clever plan to ensure that every visiting bee is dusted with pollen. Two petals at the base make a 'keel', two at the sides are called 'wings', and an upright one at the top is called 'the standard'. Within the keel, which the bee must penetrate to gain nectar, are five stamens shedding golden pollen, and a pistil. Following pollination, the ovary ripens by October to become a long black pod holding seeds like hard black peas within its leathery shell. These unpalatable pods were confused by the Pilgrim Fathers of America with the sweet and nutritious ones of the real locust tree.

Locust seedlings bear two oval seed-leaves above ground, then a few simple, undivided leaves; next, leaves with three or five leaflets, and finally typical compound leaves. The roots throw up sucker shoots, and if a locust tree is felled, a cluster of suckers will spring up around it, each striving to replace it. Heights of 32 m (104 ft) are attained, with girths up to 5.5 m (18 ft).

The timber of locust has an exceptionally decorative

Locust's pale-grey bark is very rough; thick ribs form meshwork.

character. The heartwood, which is naturally durable, has a deep golden-brown colour and attractive figure; the thin sapwood zone around it is paler. Physically this wood is tough and shock resistant, and early American settlers used it for tool handles, cart shafts, wheel spokes, ladder rungs and other items where shock resistance is important. Unfortunately locust stems bend so much that the wood is unsuited to modern sawmilling and machine wood-working. Today its main uses are for ornamental bowls, plates, and high-quality furniture.

57

WILD CHERRY

Prunus avium ROSACEAE

The wild cherry or gean tree, one of the ancestors of the garden kinds, presents a beautiful appearance at every season of the year. In winter you may know it by its remarkable purplish-grey bark, which has a metallic sheen and bears prominent rough brown lenticels, or breathing pores, ranged in horizontal bands. Its large, bright brown buds, set alternately along the stout twigs, burst in April to release long-stalked, oval leaves which have toothed edges and taper to a pointed tip. In October these leaves turn to brilliant shades of gold, orange, and scarlet-brown, before falling from the boughs.

Often the white blossoms open before the leaves, and the tree's crown appears as though caught in a late snow-drift. In other years they join the emerald-green fresh leaves to form a lovely colour harmony. These flowers are set in clusters at intervals along young branches, and each has its separate stalk. There are five green sepals, five white petals, a multitude of golden stamens, and a central pistil. They bear nectar and attract a steady stream of pollinating bees. After the petals have fallen in white drifts, each pistil ripens a single cherry fruit, which matures through green and red to black. The wild cherry has a sweet and juicy pulp, but this is too thin to merit its harvesting. In late June the birds strip the trees, sometimes swallowing the seeds, sometimes scattering them.

The hard pale-brown seed at each cherry's heart can pass unharmed through a bird's digestive system. After reaching the ground it sprouts, possibly next spring, but more likely in the spring of the year after that. The thick shell splits and two oval seed-leaves emerge, followed by an upright shoot bearing normal foliage.

Wild cherry can become a really tall tree, up to 33 m (108 ft) high. It can reach a girth of 4 m (13 ft). Large

trunks are very valuable for their decorative timber, because they can be cut into veneers that are applied as the surface finish for high-class furniture. In its solid form cherry is used for small pieces of furniture, turned bowls, table woodware such as bread-boards, and wood sculpture. It is golden brown in colour, with a paler sapwood zone. It has a lively figure, and its smooth surface is often shot through with tones of green or gold, recalling forest sunlight.

In Scotland and a few upland valleys of England and Wales grows the bird cherry, *Prunus padus*, a much smaller tree, which bears its white flowers and small black fruits along a slender stalk, and not in clusters. You may also find an occasional 'escaped' cherry growing wild, which has sprung up from some garden cherry-stone, dropped by chance, and showing the characters of a cultivated species.

Wild cherry bark is smooth and metallic grey-brown, with clear bands of corky brown breathing pores.

Rowan has purplish-brown smooth bark with shallow pore bands.

ROWAN

Sorbus aucuparia   ROSACEAE

Rowan draws its name from the old Norse word *røn*, linked perhaps with the Gaelic *ruadhan*, the red one, from its scarlet berries. It is also called the 'mountain ash', because it grows high on mountains and bears a compound leaf like an ash tree, though there are no other points of resemblance. Always a small tree, rarely exceeding 6 m (20 ft) in height, it is widely planted in suburban gardens for its lovely blossom and berries, linked with manageable size and little need for pruning.

The winter buds of rowan are distinctive. Exceptionally large, they are set singly along the twigs and have a narrow base to broad purple scales with hairy edges, ending in a pointed tip. The bark is purplish grey and always remains smooth. The timber has a red-brown heartwood surrounded by pale-brown sapwood. Too small for most purposes, it was formerly used in treeless Highland regions for tough tool handles, household utensils, such as spoons, and small furniture.

Rowan bears an attractive, feathery compound leaf, made up of numerous leaflets with deeply cut edges, set on a central stalk. The foliage turns an attractive golden-brown in autumn. In May the rowan opens clusters of short-stalked flowers, borne well clear of the foliage. Each individual flower has five green sepals, five snow-white petals, many stamens with anthers bearing golden pollen, and a central pistil. There is ample nectar to reward pollinating bees, which are attracted by the flowers' powerful, rather musky odour. The juicy berries ripen rapidly through shades of green to scarlet, and in September the birds start to strip them from the tree. Each berry has a tough orange-red outer skin, with soft yellow pulp within. Embedded in this are about six small, hard, oval yellow seeds. Birds scatter these, or swallow them, voiding them unharmed later. The seeds lie dormant for eighteen months before sprouting. A seedling rowan bears two oval seed-leaves, then simple oval true leaves and, next, leaves with only a few leaflets. The typical compound leaf appears later.

Seeds are widely spread by birds, but most seedlings are soon destroyed by grazing sheep or deer. On high mountains, therefore, rowans only survive amid the rocks and scree of crags and waterfalls, looking remarkably picturesque. Following an old superstition that rowans warded

off witches, Highland crofters often planted a rowan beside their homesteads. Many such trees survive amid the ruins of settlements deserted scores of years ago, marking their sites on the bare hills.

Rowan berries are too acid to be eaten raw, but if sugar is added their pulp can be made into rowan jelly, the best flavouring to accompany game or venison.

WHITEBEAM

Sorbus aria   ROSACEAE

This lovely tree is very common along hedgerows and small woods on the chalk downs of south and east England, and frequent on limestone soils elsewhere. But it is rare on other geological formations or north of the Scottish Lowlands. Its name includes both the old Anglo-Saxon word 'beam' for tree, and the white appearance of its leaves. This colour arises from a coating of hairs on the underside of each leaf, which helps to lessen water loss on the dry, freely-draining soils where it grows. Whiteness is first seen in April when the leaves expand in goblet-shaped groups, resembling large tulips ornamenting the branches. Throughout the summer it is only revealed when wind stirs the foliage, for the upper side of each leaf, exposed to the sun, is mid-green. The poet Meredith recalls this in the lines:

> *Flashing as in gusts*
> *The sudden-lighted whitebeam.*

In autumn, when the upper sides of the leaves turn dark brown, the white colour still persists, even on leaves that have fallen to the forest floor.

Whitebeam has a grey bark that remains smooth save on very old trees, where shallow flakes and fissures appear. Its timber has a pale creamy-brown sapwood and a mid-brown inner heartwood. It is strong and stable and can be worked to a smooth finish, but large trees are so scarce that there is no regular market. Some of its wood is used, however, for turned bowls and plates, and small decorative woodware.

The flowers open in May, in showy clusters. Each has five green sepals, five white petals, many stamens and a central pistil that ripens, later on, into a yellow berry holding several small hard seeds. These seeds, spread by

64

Old whitebeams develop spiral cracks in smooth grey bark.

birds, lie dormant in the soil for eighteen months before germinating. The seedling bears two seed-leaves, followed by typical simple oval leaves. The tallest common whitebeam is 16 m (52 ft) high, and the stoutest has a girth of 2 m (6 ft).

Whitebeam is closely related to the rowan, and where the two trees grow side by side they often interbreed, producing a hybrid called the Swedish whitebeam, *Sorbus intermedia*. This has pinnately lobed leaves with toothed edges, a pattern midway between those of its two parents. Similar hybrids are planted in parks or as street trees because of their rapid growth to medium size, combined with attractive foliage, flowers and fruit, and exceptional resistance to town smoke.

HAWTHORN

Crataegus monogyna   ROSACEAE

Hawthorn has become the commonest small tree over most of England, and much of Scotland, Ireland and Wales, because of its value for stock-proof hedges. When the old open fields were enclosed to make modern farms, mainly between 1650 and 1850, wire was too costly for fences and stone too scarce in many districts. Farmers therefore planted countless miles of small hawthorn plants, and protected them from cattle with temporary wood fences till they grew stout. They have maintained the resulting tough hedge ever since by regular lopping, laying slanting stems, and reinforcing weak spots with stakes. Many bushes are therefore over 100 or even 200 years old.

If left unlopped, hawthorn becomes a small tree with a rounded crown, seldom more than 6 m (20 ft) tall. Its bark has a purplish to rusty-brown colour, breaking away in squarish flakes, and the small trunk is always irregular, never neatly round. The black twigs are thin and tough and bear, at intervals, the sharp black thorns that give the tree its name. These thorns help to check wandering cattle or sheep. Early in April the minute buds break, showing yellow-brown bud-scales, and release bright emerald-green leaves. These turn dark green later and become dull brown before falling in autumn. Each leaf has an irregular pinnately lobed outline, the mainly oval shape being divided by deep recesses.

Hawthorn flowers, also called 'may blossom', open in showy clusters, crowding the branches of trees that have not been lopped. They are usually white and single, but in gardens many strains with red, pink or double white flowers are grown; these are usually grafted on stocks of the common kind. Each separate flower has five green sepals, five white or coloured petals, a cluster of stamens and a central pistil. Pollination is effected by bees which are attracted by the flowers' bold display, strong musky perfume, and abundant nectar. They dust pollen from male stamens on to receptive female stigmas, usually on another tree.

The familiar berries, called haws, ripen in October as groups of fleshy crimson-brown fruits, each bearing the woody remnants of the five sepals at its tip. Within their pulp lies the seed, a hard stone. Birds strip the trees in winter, often swallowing the stone and voiding it, unharmed, later. To raise hawthorn seedlings, nurserymen gather ripe berries, and store them in moist sand for eighteen months, for they will not sprout earlier. The

Rough barked and reddish grey, hawthorn trunks develop distinct flutes, often spirally inclined.

seed-leaves remain in the husk, which sends up a shoot bearing normal foliage.

Hawthorn wood has a rusty-brown heartwood and a pale-brown outer sapwood. It is strong and tough but too small for any real use, except as hedge stakes.

ASH

Fraxinus excelsior   OLEACEÀE

Ash grows as a native tree throughout the British Isles, and is particularly vigorous on limestone rocks, since it tolerates calcium in the soil. Its common name is derived from Scandinavian *ask* and Anglo-Saxon *aesc*. Ash grows readily from self-set, wind-blown seed, but as its leaves attract grazing livestock, seedlings get bitten back on pastures. A few survive in rock crevices that sheep cannot reach.

Ash bears a typical ash-grey bark, smooth at first, which gradually develops a regular meshwork of raised ribs, like a fishing-net. Its branching crown is always open, with ample space between separate limbs and twigs. It may grow to 45 m (148 ft) tall, but its girth can only reach 6.7 m (22 ft) and its age seldom exceeds 150 years.

Very hard, jet-black, dull-surfaced buds, set in opposite pairs on slightly flattened, greenish-grey twigs, make ash unmistakable in winter. They open, later than nearly all other trees, late in April, to release distinctive leaves. On its long stalk, each compound leaf, up to 15 cm (6 in.) long, carries about seven pairs of oval opposite leaflets, plus a terminal leaflet at its tip. The edges of leaflets carry short teeth. Leaves fade to grey brown and fall, all in one piece, in October.

The flower clusters of ash open early in May, just as the leaves are expanding, and can be seen as green tassels or catkins on the twigs. Separate flowers, which lack sepals and petals, may bear either male stamens, or female pistils, or possibly organs of both sexes together. Pollination is effected by wind. Male flowers have two small green stamens and female ones a short green pistil that later ripens a single seed. By September the clusters of green ripening seeds show up on the branches, and in

October they turn brown and fall. Ash seeds are called 'keys' because they resemble keys used for medieval locks. Each has a single, twisted wing that keeps it airborne until it has drifted away from its parent tree on the autumn wind.

Seedlings bear first two oval, smooth, green seed-leaves, then a few oval, tooth-edged simple leaves; next, leaves with only three leaflets and finally compound leaves like their parents.

The wood of ash has an even pale creamy-brown colour. It is easily recognized by annual rings with distinct

Grey ash bark forms a lovely symmetrical network of ribs and hollows.

pores; these are vessels developed in spring for quick transport of sap. Later, each summer, ash forms a ring of denser wood, which makes it very strong, tough and resistant to shock. It is preferred above all other native timbers for the handles of hammers, axes, shovels, chisels, and all tools subject to sudden shocks and strains. It is favoured for hockey sticks, oars, and similar tough sports equipment. Traditional uses include cart shafts and the rims of cart-wheels, subject to hard jolts. Ash is also used for attractive furniture, bowls and small ornaments.

COMMON ELM

Ulmus procera   ULMACEAE

The common or English elm, also called the 'field elm', is the finest of several varieties that flourish in the lowlands of the British Isles. It is seen most frequently along hedgerows, and its presence there is often due to deliberate schemes of planting by 18th-century landowners. When the old open fields were being enclosed by tenant farmers, using hawthorn hedges, the landowners required

Common elm's dark grey-brown bark shows broken, shallow, wandering ribs.

them to plant elms, for timber, shade and shelter, at intervals. These elms were raised, as offshoots from a common stock, in nurseries, which explains why trees over a wide area have identical characters. They rarely set fertile seed, but sucker shoots spring vigorously from their roots, to replace mature trees felled for timber.

Common elm grows fast to become a very tall tree, up to 45 m (147 ft) high and 8 m (26 ft) round. Its rough, grey-brown bark is broken into distinct squarish plates. Stout twigs bear alternately set, oval, dark-brown buds.

Leaves have an oval outline, a toothed edge and a pointed tip. Their surface, rough to the touch, shows clear parallel veins; emerald-green in spring, they darken later and turn bright golden-brown in autumn. A distinctive feature is their oblique or uneven leaf base, different on the two sides.

Elm flowers in February, opening clusters of catkins high on leafless branches, where they are seen distantly as a dull crimson haze. Each wind-pollinated flower has three basal green bracts, a six-lobed calyx of green sepals, six stamens with purplish-crimson anthers and a central pistil with two stigmas. Fertilized flowers mature quickly to make conspicuous bunches of winged seeds, ripening in April, just as the leaves open. People often mistake these seeds for flowers, or even for foliage. Each tiny seed lies at the centre of a pale-green papery wing, which aids its dispersal by wind.

Elm seeds can only sprout if they alight on damp soil within a few weeks of ripening. The seedling, seldom seen, bears two oval seed-leaves, then normal foliage.

Elm timber has a pale, cream-coloured sapwood and a rich brown heartwood that shows, on all cut surfaces, an intricate pattern of light and dark tissues. Though not durable out of doors near ground level, it will last for centuries if kept dry or, alternatively, always wet, as in a buried water-pipe. Its tough interlocked grain makes it virtually impossible to split, and it was long used for purposes where metals are now applied. Examples are wheel-hubs, ships' keels, chair seats, water-pipes made by hollowing out whole tree trunks, and water pumps. Today it is mainly used for sturdy, attractive furniture, and coffins.

For Dutch elm disease, *see* pages 77–78.

WYCH ELM

Ulmus glabra   ULMACEAE

This beautiful tree, also known as 'Scots elm', is only
common as a native tree in Scotland and northern England. Elsewhere it is widely planted for ornament, because of its gracefully spreading crown. There is an
unusual weeping variety, *U.* 'Pendula', in which all the
branches bend downwards to form a green dome. This is
always grafted on the upright stock of another elm, to
give it the necessary height. Unlike the other European
elms, wych elm grows readily from seed, but does not
send up sucker shoots. It is frequent in woodlands,
thriving on the slopes of rocky glens, but scarce along
hedgerows.

The bark of wych elm shows a handsome symmetrical
network of shallow ribs, pale grey in colour. The trunk
nearly always divides low down into large spreading
limbs, which makes the timber awkward for sawmillers to
handle. Nevertheless wych elm wood is highly valued for
toughness and supple strength, particularly in boat-build-
ing. Much is also used for furniture. It has a pale-brown,
almost white, sapwood, with a dark-brown inner heartwood.

Wych elm can be told apart from other elms by its
stouter twigs which bear, at distinct angles, single, large,
oval chestnut-brown buds. Its leaves are larger, too, and
have markedly uneven bases. Oval in general outline,
they taper abruptly to a clear tip. Their veins are strongly
marked, their edges toothed, and their surfaces remarkably rough to the touch.

Wych elm flowers resemble those of common elm but
are larger. Seeds are set at the centres of large, leaf-like
green wings. When they ripen in late April, just before
the pale-green leaves break, the elms, especially the
weeping ones, appear clad in foliage already. Then the

wind scatters the seeds, and a few that alight on moist earth or in rock crevices sprout during early summer. The tallest recorded wych elm reaches 44 m (144 ft), the stoutest is 8 m (26 ft) round.

Wych elm has proved relatively resistant to, though not immune from, the Dutch elm disease that has resulted in serious loss among elms of all kinds. This disease is so called because, though believed to originate on more resistant elms in eastern Europe, it first caused major damage, around 1927, in Holland. It is brought about

On wych elm the grey ribs are thicker, and their trend more directly vertical.

by a minute fungus, *Ceratocystis ulmi*, which grows in the outermost annual ring of wood that the tree forms each summer. It blocks the flow of sap and kills a high proportion of trees attacked. The fungus is spread by little black beetles, *Scolytus scolytus*, which feed on the bark and bast of weakened trees; they carry fungal spores on their bodies, which infect healthy elms. Both fungus and beetle are almost impossible to check by direct means, so tree growers hope that strains of elm immune to the disease will soon be found.

PLANE

Platanus × *hispanica*   PLATANACEAE

Plane trees are usually first recognized by their dappled bark, for as each segment of olive-brown bark ages, it flakes off and exposes a creamy-white surface below. This turns green and later brown. Bark shedding definitely helps the plane to thrive in smoky cities, for trees must breathe in oxygen through bark as well as leaves.

79

Plane twigs take a zigzag course and bear, at each angle and at their tip, green, conical, pointed buds shaped like a dunce's cap. The leaves are alternately set, a clear contrast with the opposite leaves of the similar European sycamore, *Acer pseudoplatanus*. Each long leaf-stalk holds a deep conical hollow at its base, in which next season's bud develops. The leaf-blade is palmately lobed; its broad surface bears several points, each linked to the stalk by a strong vein. Mid-green in summer, the leaves fade to brown in autumn.

In May, planes bear green, wind-pollinated, catkin-like flower-heads, of separate sexes, though both look alike. These clusters hang down on long stalks, usually with a second one below the first, and are aptly called 'bobbles'. Each round male flower-head is a compact mass of little blossoms, each consisting of four upright anthers, set on a green base; stamens scatter yellow pollen. The little female flowers, crowded on a female 'bobble', have each a ring of short green sepals and petals, topped by clusters of pistils bearing crimson styles. Fruits ripen next winter, turning brown and slowly breaking up. Each fruiting bobble releases scores of tiny seeds bearing short hairs to aid dispersal by wind. Many people find these hairs irritating.

Plane seedlings are seldom seen, since most seed is infertile. Each has a pair of long, narrow seed-leaves, followed by oval juvenile leaves, which are succeeded in turn by normal lobed ones. The timber of plane is pale reddish brown in colour, without clear distinction of heartwood. Strong, though not durable out of doors, it is applied to indoor purposes such as furniture and decorative carving and turnery, as in trays, bowls and ornaments. If cut at a tangent to the log's circumference, it shows a beautiful, intricate pattern of ray tissues, and the resulting timber is sold as 'lacewood'.

The plane we usually see is the London plane, *Platanus × hispanica*, which arose as a chance hybrid between two foreign trees, possibly at Oxford, in about 1670. One parent is the oriental plane, *P. orientalis*, from Turkey, the other the American plane, *P. occidentalis*, from the eastern United States. London plane shows marked hybrid vigour, quick growth and resistance to pests or diseases. Since its seed is seldom fertile, it is increased by cuttings or layers. It is widely planted as a shade tree in London parks and other great cities. Some trees are already 300 years old; our tallest so far reaches 38 m (125 ft) and our stoutest is 8.2 m (27 ft) round.

Plane shows dappled bark, yellow, olive-green and grey, due to old dark plates falling away and revealing young pale bark below.

WALNUT

Juglans regia   JUGLANDACEAE

Walnut was introduced by the Romans. Its name, originally Anglo-Saxon, means strange or foreign nut. This
delicious seed gives ample reason for its cultivation in
Roman villa gardens. At first sight walnut resembles ash,
but the ribs and fissures of its pale-grey bark are more
broadly patterned. The leaves are placed alternately on
the twigs, not opposite, and each compound leaf has
rounded leaflets, not pointed ones. If you crush a walnut
leaf, the rich aroma at once reveals the tree's identity.
The juice will stain your fingers brown – gypsies use it
as a suntan lotion! Note the round buds on the sturdy
twigs. If you slice a twig across, at an angle, you will see
that its otherwise hollow pith is crossed by little plates,
like ladder rungs.

In May, soon after the leaves have opened, walnut
opens male and female flowers of quite different patterns,
at separate points in leaf axils. The male catkins are
drooping green structures, rather like caterpillars, which
scatter wind-borne pollen. Each holds numerous flowers,
composed individually of one bract, two bracteoles, four
sepals, and about fifteen stamens. The small green flowers,
solitary or grouped in twos, threes or fours, stand upright
and resemble Italian wine-flasks in shape. They bear two
recurved stigmas. After pollination the ovary at the base
of each flower expands to form a green fruit, with a thick
leathery skin. This is the 'green walnut' which, if plucked
in August, and steeped in vinegar, makes a strongly
flavoured pickle.

If walnuts are left to ripen fully, the green husk
withers away, and the actual nut becomes fully exposed
in October. This now has a hard, wrinkled, pale-brown
shell. Within lies the delicious kernel, made up of two
wrinkled seed-leaves with a papery brown film between

them, though they unite at one point. This oily kernel is nutritious, too, and orchards of high-yielding strains are tended under sunny climates to produce commercial crops. If sown next spring, a walnut sends up a sturdy shoot that bears leaves with only three leaflets; normal ones follow.

Walnut timber has a pale-brown sapwood and a deep-brown inner heartwood, shot through with veins and blotches of darker and paler shades of brown, grey and black. It is strong and naturally durable, though rarely used out of doors. Its attractive appearance, firmness,

Walnut bark bears thick grey ribs with shiny flat faces.

and smooth surface ensure its use in wood sculpture, carving turnery and ornamental work, including trays and bowls. Because it is very stable, it is used for all good gun-stocks. Large stems are sliced into veneers, applied to decorate high-grade furniture of many kinds. Solid walnut furniture is costly and rare.

The tallest walnut reaches 25 m (82 ft). The stoutest is 6.7 m (22 ft) round.

BIRCHES

Betula pendula   BETULACEAE
B. pubescens
B. nana

Birches are graceful native trees, found throughout the British Isles. The common or silver birch, *B. pendula*, has smooth twigs bearing little swellings or warts, while the less frequent hairy birch, *B. pubescens*, has downy twigs. In the far north of Scotland you may find the dwarf birch, *B. nana*.

The beautiful white bark of birch often develops diamond-shaped black patches.

All birches bear exceptionally thin, dark purplish-brown twigs; many droop gracefully. They carry alternately set, minute, dark-scaled buds, which open in April to release long-stalked leaves. These have toothed edges and a variable outline, being triangular, oval or sometimes diamond shaped, but always ending in a pointed tip. They are tinged brown when they are open, but soon become pale green, then dark green; they turn yellow before falling in October.

As the dark twigs of birch expand into stouter branches, their bark cambium develops a beautiful white covering of fresh bark, a clear distinguishing feature. Later on, near the base of large old trees, and locally up the trunk, wrinkles of dark, black bark may appear. Birch never becomes a very large tree; heights of 31 m (102 ft) and girths of 3.7 m (12 ft) approach its maximum. Nor does it live long. The birch polypore fungus, *Polyporus betulinus*, which produces conspicuous, creamy-white, bracket-shaped sporophores projecting from its trunk, often rots its inner timber, causing downfall after only sixty years' growth.

In winter the future male catkins of birch may be seen as small grey-brown sausage-shaped structures on the twigs. In April they expand and droop down as pretty 'lamb's tails'. Each holds a series of tiny flowers grouped in clusters of three below a bract; each individual flower consists of three smaller bracts and four stamens. After shedding their abundant bright yellow pollen, the male catkins fade and fall. The associated female catkins only become apparent in April. They are green, horizontal or upright structures, studded with prickly bracts, about 1.25 cm ($\frac{1}{2}$ in.) long, and resemble caterpillars. Below each bract stands a group of three flowers, each an ovary bearing two stigmas. These catkins ripen quickly through the summer to become larger, oval, seeding catkins, which break up in October to release scores of tiny winged seeds together with little three-lobed bracts. The wind carries

birch seeds everywhere, and seedlings sprout from damp earth next spring in all sorts of odd spots. Foresters rarely plant birch, since all they need springs from self-sown seed. They are more likely to weed it out to save other trees! Each seedling bears two small, oval, opposite seed-leaves, then alternate, triangular or three-lobed primary leaves, and next normal foliage.

Birch timber is pale brown in colour and always shows a dull, matt surface with no apparent annual rings, distinct heartwood or other attractive features. Strong and tough, though not durable out of doors, it is used where appearance matters little, for example, as short tool handles, broom-heads, and cheap kitchen furniture. It is a first-rate fire-wood.

ALDER

Alnus glutinosa   BETULACEAE

Alder, a widespread native tree, is nearly always found on the banks of streams, rivers and lakes, or in places where water formerly stood or ran. Its tiny seeds are water-borne by little floats, and only sprout readily on damp mud.

Alder has a dark-grey or black bark, broken into irregular squares by fissures. Its twigs are stout and ridged, greyish brown with a purplish bloom. Each alternately set bud has a good distinguishing point, a distinct constriction or 'stalk' at its base. The leaves, opening in April, have a rounded outline, toothed edges, strong veins, and a blunt or notched tip. Mid-green at first, they darken later, and turn dull brown before falling early in November.

Male catkins are visible through the winter as brown oval bodies. In March they expand and droop in 'lamb's tail' shapes, exposing many clusters of simple flowers, each having four stamens and four petals. Purplish brown, they scatter showers of golden pollen, which the wind wafts through leafless boughs, then wither and fall. The female catkins, previously seen as small, green, short-stalked clubs, now expand to catch the pollen on the two stigmas that each single, simple flower holds. Each flower is merely a female pistil, without petals.

During the summer the female catkins expand to become 'cones', the alder's most distinctive feature. These cones resemble those of conifers, but since they differ structurally and show no close botanical relationship, they are usually called 'false cones'. Green at first, they become hard and woody by autumn. Each scale, a modified bract, bears one little seed. Empty cones persist on leafless twigs through winter, making alder easy to recognize at this time. Each seed bears floats which aid water dispersal, though some seeds are spread by wind or by ducks with muddy feet! The little seedlings bear two, paired, triangular seed-leaves, then normal foliage.

Alder roots bear swellings called nodules, in which lives a bacterium, *Schinzia alni*, which enables the alder to 'fix' the valuable nutrient nitrogen from the air. Where alders cover swampy ground, called a 'carr' in many districts, their leaf-fall enriches the soil, making clearance and draining profitable for farmers.

Never a large tree, alder can reach 21 m (70 ft) tall, with girths up to 4.3 m (14 ft). Most trees have been

Alder bark is dark grey, and very rugged.

lopped in the past to harvest poles but sometimes also to clear river-banks for boating, fishing, or the passage of draining machines. Alder poles have three traditional uses. They are a good turnery wood, and round tool handles and half-round broom-heads are still made. Being easily carved, yet tough and water resistant, they made the best soles for wooden shoes or clogs. When turned into charcoal, they give first-rate gunpowder. An odd feature of the wood is that, when freshly exposed, its sapwood turns bright orange. Alder bark was once used for tanning leather.

HORNBEAM

Carpinus betulus   BETULACEAE

Hornbeam draws its name, a compound of 'horn' and the
old Anglo-Saxon word 'beam', meaning a tree, from its
very hard, strong, smooth white wood. This was used in
the past for ox-yokes and the cog-wheels of water-mills
and windmills, before metals had been developed. Its main
use today is in butchers' chopping-blocks, for when set in
small squares, with the end of the grain uppermost, it
withstands cutting better than any other timber.

Though native, hornbeam reached Britain later than other common trees, and did not naturally spread far from the south and east. Its northern and western limits are roughly those of the upper Thames Valley, with outliers in South Wales. Locally in the south-east hornbeam is common, because woods were deliberately planted for coppicing, that is, repeated cutting back to the tree-stump, to yield fire-wood and faggots, which are bundles of dry twigs used as fire-lighters or to heat bakers' ovens. In Epping Forest and locally elsewhere the hornbeams were lopped 2 m (6 ft) up, so that cattle could not eat their young shoots: such trees are called 'pollards'.

At first sight most people mistake hornbeam for beech, but a few pointers show the differences. Hornbeam's bark, though smooth and grey, carries irregular strands of a paler bright metallic colour. Its trunk has wandering ribs, running outside the main cylinder, called 'flutes'. The alternately set buds are shorter than those of beech, and bend inwards towards the twig. The leaves, pale green and oval as in beech, can be told by much clearer veins and a distinctly toothed edge. In winter they turn brilliant yellow, then fade to pale brown. Those on low branches remain attached to the twigs all winter, and this makes hornbeam an attractive hedge shrub.

Hornbeam bears separate male and female catkins, both unlike those of beech, which open in April. Male catkins hang down in 'lamb's tail' formation, each main stalk carrying clusters of little flowers, set below oval bracts. Each cluster is technically three flowers, with four stamens apiece. They shed pollen, after which the whole catkin fades and falls. The much smaller female catkins are groups of small green flowers hidden amid leafy bracts at branch-tips. These female flowers, set in pairs, each have a pistil and three bracteoles. By September they have ripened to characteristic hanging fruit catkins, with many fruits on each stalk. Each fruit consists of a large papery brown wing, having a big central lobe and two smaller side lobes. At the centre stands the little seed or nutlet. This is big enough to attract the mice, squirrels and birds that help to spread those seeds they fail to eat. The wings carry other seeds on the wind. Hornbeam seedlings bear two oval seed-leaves, followed by heart-shaped early leaves with irregular edges, then normal foliage.

Though seldom a large tree, hornbeam may grow 32 m (105 ft) tall and up to 5 m (17 ft) round.

Hornbeam has a fluted trunk, clad in metallic grey, smooth bark.

HAZEL

Corylus avellana   BETULACEAE

Hazel, found in all parts of the British Isles, is always a
woody bush, up to 6 m (20 ft) tall, rather than a single-
stemmed tree. It branches freely and has amazing powers
of regeneration when it is cut back. This process, called
coppicing, from Norman French *couper*, to cut, was prac-
tised in all districts to ensure repeated supplies of thin
rods and poles. Hazel rods were used for weaving hurdles
and 'dead hedges', as the 'wattle' of wattle-and-daub
buildings, for rough baskets, and as spars to hold thatch
on cottage roofs and corn ricks. Hazel also provided pea
sticks, bean rods, faggots for kindling, and fire-wood.
Nowadays, when demands for all these things have
diminished, most coppices are neglected. Some have become game coverts and others are nature reserves.

Hazel is known in winter by branchy, rather hairy
twigs, carrying alternate round greenish buds. The leaves,
opening in April, are large rounded oblongs with a doubly
toothed edge. Though broader towards the tip, they end
in a central point. In late October they turn yellow and
fall. Hazel bark is very smooth, and mottled in shades of
brown and grey.

Male catkins can be seen as groups of grey-brown oval
bodies all winter through. In February, well ahead of the
leaves, they expand to become drooping 'lamb's tails',
bright with golden pollen, which are often picked for
decoration. Each catkin holds many groups of male
flowers on its long hanging stem. There are many flowers
in each group, and each has four stamens on a single
scale. These male catkins fade and fall in March. The
tiny female catkins are difficult to find. They are little
green bud-shaped structures scattered along the twigs,
and may be known by their short crimson stigmas, which
catch wind-borne pollen. Hidden within each bud is a

single flower, with a solitary pistil surrounded by green bracts.

During summer the female flowers expand into nuts, which turn brown and ripen by October. Each nut sits within a leafy husk that has developed from the bracts. The nuts have hard shells to protect their large, nutritious

kernels, which have a brown skin and white flesh. Selected strains of hazels and related filberts are grown for nut crops in Kent, and great quantities are imported for use in chocolate and confectionery. In the woods most of the nuts get eaten by birds such as pheasants, pigeons and jays, or by sharp-toothed squirrels and dormice. When the few survivors sprout next spring the seed-leaves remain within the nutshell. The first shoot carries a few small, scale-like, juvenile leaves, then normal foliage.

Hazel stools bear many stems, clad in smooth grey bark with distinct breathing pores.

PEDUNCULATE AND SESSILE OAKS

Quercus robur and *Quercus petraea*　　　　FAGACEAE

Pedunculate oak (*Quercus robur*) is the commoner of two
species that are widespread throughout most of Europe,
including the British Isles. It is distinguished by having
its female flowers, and the acorns that develop from them,
set on long stalks or 'peduncles'. Its leaves, by contrast,
are short stalked or stalkless; they also bear lobes, called
'auricles', on either side at their base. The second species,
called sessile oak (*Q. petraea*), has *stalkless acorns*, and
long-stalked leaves, lacking basal lobes. Our illustrations
show the critical differences between the two kinds; but
hybrids between the two, showing intermediate characters, are common.

A constant feature of all the oaks is the grouping of
buds towards the tip of each twig; this makes them easy
to recognize both in summer and winter. This bud pattern
gives rise to bunched leaves, and also causes the rugged
arrangement of the oak's branches. Scattered solitary buds
also appear along the twigs, farther down.

Oak leaves show a characteristic pinnately lobed
pattern, with irregular rounded lobes projecting on
either side of a central mid-rib. They have smooth un-
toothed edges and a rounded tip. Pale green when they
open in April, they become a rich mid-green by mid-
summer. Late in October they fade to a dull, or sometimes a bright golden-brown. A remarkable feature of
vigorous oaks is their second, late summer outburst of
foliage, which is called 'Lammas growth' after Lammas
Day, 1st August. Long shoots then develop, carrying
fresh leaves which are, at first, crimson rather than
green.

The flowers of oak are wind-pollinated catkins which
open in May. Male catkins, set at intervals on the twigs,
are groups of long hanging stalks that bear, dispersed

along them, simple yellow flowers. Each flower has a basal bract, six green sepals and eight yellow stamens. These tassels of male flowers soon fade and fall. Female flowers are set separately along the same twigs, in groups of two or three. Each has a green bract, numerous bracteoles, and a central pistil. Following the pollination of an ovule within the ovary at the base of the pistil, the whole female flower structure develops rapidly. Soft green bracteoles unite, turn woody and become, by September, the familiar acorn cup, dark green and scaly without, smooth and brown within.

The acorn is so called from old Danish words *eg korn*, meaning oak seed. Each flower ripens a single acorn, which is really a large oval nut, with a hard, smooth, brown skin. Acorns of pedunculate oak have blunt, swollen ends, whereas those of sessile oak are conical, tapering towards their tips. Inside the husk are two hard, swollen, white seed-leaves or cotyledons. These never function as green leaves, but remain within the shell, serving as food stores for the seedling. In spring this sends up a sturdy shoot that bears first a few small green bracts, then normal leaves.

Good crops of acorns occur only at intervals of a few years, in 'mast' years, from Scandinavian *mat* meaning food. Though too acid for people to eat, acorns are welcome food for squirrels, wood mice, pheasants, jays, woodpeckers and wood-pigeons. Though most get eaten, a few always survive to sprout next spring. Jays regularly carry them to open ground and bury them in turf as a winter food store. Those they forget become oaks! In the past, and even today in the New Forest, acorns formed a valued food for fattening pigs. After a good acorn crop, these animals are turned loose to forage throughout the autumn. This is still called the 'pannage' season, from Norman French *pesner*, meaning 'to grub with the snout'.

Oak bark is smooth and greyish brown in young twigs, but develops a characteristic pattern as branches expand.

Sessile oak   **Pedunculate oak**

Its rough grey surface is broken into small irregular
squares by deep fissures, some more or less vertical,
others mainly horizontal. Bark stripped from felled logs
was formerly widely used for tanning hides to turn them
into leather.

The outer, thin, sapwood zone of an oak stem is pale
yellow in colour. After the tree is felled it proves perishable, rotting in a few years → although whilst the tree is

99

still alive it may support a crown of branches above an old decayed and hollow trunk.

By contrast, the dark-brown inner heartwood, rich in the tannin which resists fungi, is remarkably durable once the tree has been felled. This 'heart of oak' endures for scores of years when used as a fence post or the keel of a wooden ship, or for centuries as a beam or rafter in a building, or as any sort of indoor furniture. Running right through the whole stem are distinct ray tissues, seen on cross-sections as thin bright lines radiating from the centre, and on some longitudinal surfaces as shining plates – the lovely 'silver grain' of oak panelling.

The uses of oak follow its unique properties of great strength and durability, linked to attractive appearance. They include fencing, the building of timber barns and half-timbered houses, churches, and ships of many kinds – from Viking long ships and Nelson's battleships to modern fishing craft on Scotland's stormy seaboards. Oak tables, chests and chairs are used in the home, and oak is the traditional timber for joinery in public buildings, church pews, pulpits and similar high-class and durable woodwork. Oak is always chosen for the staves of beer barrels and sherry casks, for the spokes of wooden wheels, and the rungs of strong ladders.

In practice, timber users make no distinction between the wood of pedunculate oak and that of sessile oak. Rate of growth is more important. Strangely enough, *fast-grown* oak holds proportionately more strong summerwood than slow-grown oak, and is therefore *stronger*.

Sessile oak, reputedly the straighter tree, can reach a height of 41 m (135 ft) and a girth of 13 m (43 ft). Records for pedunculate oak are 37 m (120 ft) tall and 9 m (30 ft) round. Our oldest oaks have stood for over 1000 years. All these veterans have been pollarded, that is, lopped for fire-wood, a process that prolongs their life-span, and most now have decayed and hollow centres.

Oakwoods, either pure or mixed with other trees, form

Pedunculate oak bears grey bark of great character surfaced by irregular ribs.

the natural native forest cover over most of the better soils in the lowlands of the British Isles. Both sessile and pedunculate oaks have been widely planted, to yield timber or improve the landscape. Owing to their crowded buds, young oak saplings grow at first like straggly bushes, but eventually one shoot takes the lead and a tall straight main stem develops. An oak's crown of branches always tends to become broad, even in a crowded forest. This feature is more marked in the open, especially along hedgerows and with pollard trees that were once lopped for fire-wood.

The woods of poor, stunted, mis-shaped oaks found in many highland districts are the outcome of coppicing, and do not represent natural growth. For centuries they were cut back, every twenty years or so, to yield fencing and building timbers from their stouter stems, fire-wood and charcoal wood from their thinner ones, and valuable bark for tanning leather. Several crooked stems then sprouted from each stump, and the coppicing process was later repeated.

Another type of oak to look for is the 'standard tree', which was carefully preserved as a sapling over a coppice crop of hazel, hornbeam or sweet chestnut until, after a hundred years of growth, it was stout enough to yield large sturdy beams valuable for building houses, barns or bridges.

TURKEY OAK

Quercus cerris   FAGACEAE

This is a tree to look for in parks, or odd corners of woods in the grounds of great estates. Introduced from Turkey as a promising timber tree, and widely planted for ornament, it has become naturalized in many districts. Jays, which carry acorns of all kinds and bury them, are probably responsible for its spread.

103

At first sight this tree looks like a pedunculate oak, with an unusually straight and vigorous main trunk. A close look at the rough grey bark may reveal a curious key feature: the deep fissures show a bright tangerine-orange colour. Turkey oak's leaves are pinnately lobed like those of other common sorts, but the lobes have a markedly 'stepped' outline, somewhat like saw-teeth. At the base of each leaf-stalk there are several long slender bracts called stipules.

The acorn cups of Turkey oak are clad in curious leafy outgrowths, which have earned it the name of 'moss-cupped oak'. The acorns themselves are large, and oblong rather than oval, with blunt tips.

Unfortunately, the attractive timber that Turkey oak produces relatively fast in its well-shaped stem has, in Britain, no commercial value. Timber merchants have long avoided it, and trials at the Princes Risborough Laboratory of the Building Research Establishment confirm their view that it shrinks, warps and twists more than other hardwood. Yet, the Turks, with their different climate, find their home-grown oak timber very serviceable.

The tallest Turkey oak recorded in Britain is 37 m (120 ft) tall, while the stoutest measures 8.2 m (27 ft) round.

Turkey oak is one of the parents of the hybrid Lucombe oak, *Quercus* × *hispanica* var. *lucombeana*, first found in 1765 by an Exeter nurseryman named Lucombe. This is a vigorous ornamental tree with a sub-evergreen habit; it holds its glossy, dark-green lobed leaves through the winter, but they fall in spring. Its other parent is the Mediterranean cork oak, *Q. suber*, a true evergreen that is barely hardy, even in the south of England. Cork oak has the unique property of withstanding the removal of its outer bark, a process that kills any other tree. Fresh layers of thick soft bark grow again after each stripping, which is done at intervals of about twenty years. This

104

is the cork universally used for floats, heat insulation and waterproof and spirit-proof bottle-stoppers.

Another oak that you may find in parks and woods is the American red oak, *Q. borealis*, which has pointed lobes to its leaves, giving them a flame-shaped outline. These dark-green leaves have always a reddish tinge, and in autumn they change to vivid shades of crimson, scarlet and orange.

Turkey oak shows long, rougher ribs, forming a haphazard network; orange tints in fissures.

HOLM OAK

Quercus ilex   FAGACEAE

At first sight the holm oak looks like a giant holly; 'holm'
is an old local name for the latter tree. It is one of a large
group of trees and shrubs that are specially adapted to
live in countries with hot dry summers and cool rainy
winters – a 'Mediterranean' climate – and the holm oak
originates in the countries around the Mediterranean

Holm oak's black bark shows many small, shallow oblongs.

Sea. Similar evergreen oaks are found in California and the south-eastern states of the U.S.A.

Holm oak retains its leaves through winter to make use of available rainwater. They have a thick leathery texture that enables them to resist summer drought. Oval in shape, with pointed tips, they are dark glossy green above and pale grey beneath, with inrolled edges, which are usually smooth but occasionally toothed. Each leaf lives for about three years, eventually becoming dark

107

brown and hard before it falls. In spring pale-green shoots grow out from the dark foliage mass to extend the tree's crown. During a hard winter all the leaves may turn brown, but they recover green shades next spring.

The bark of holm oak is dark grey to black, broken into a multitude of rough-surfaced, small, irregular squares. The trunk beneath it has a narrow, pale, outer sapwood zone, and a central heartwood that is exceptionally hard, close-grained and heavy. It is used for decorative woodware, in the framing of ships or machinery where great strength is needed, and more generally as a first-rate fire-wood.

Because it resists salt-laden winds off the sea, holm oak has been planted as a shelter-belt tree near several south coast towns. Here and there it has become naturalized on waste land, including poor chalk downlands on the Isle of Wight. Individual trees can reach a height of 30 m (98 ft) and girths up to 6.7 m (22 ft).

Male catkins resemble those of pedunculate oak, with flowers of a greyer colour. Female catkins have long stalks topped by three or four separate, bud-shaped flowers; but as a rule only one flower matures to yield an acorn. A holm oak acorn has an oval form, tapering to a bluntly pointed tip. It grows enclosed for over half its length in a deep cup with grey scales, and is itself olive-brown in colour. Pigs and birds eat the acorns readily.

The striking, prominent ribs of brown sweet chestnut bark form a network, often spiral.

SWEET CHESTNUT

Castanea sativa FAGACEAE

Sweet chestnut, native to southern Europe, was introduced to Britain by the Romans, possibly around A.D. 100. They used its nutritious nuts, and a flour made from them called *polenta*, as staple rations for their legionary soldiers, and sought to raise supplies here. Sweet chestnut bears ripe seed only in southern Britain, and then not every

109

year. It has become naturalized locally in the New Forest and the Forest of Dean, but elsewhere is usually planted.

Sweet chestnut is easily known by its bold, ribbed, purplish-brown twigs, which bear large, round, alternately set buds at long intervals. Its leaves, exceptionally large, grow up to 25 cm (10 in.) long. They have a long oval outline, and their edges are boldly toothed, like the teeth of a saw. Pale green when they open in April, they become darker later and fade to golden hues in October.

In June sweet chestnut opens curious catkins, bearing both male and female flowers on one stalk. The male flowers are clusters of golden stamens, set along its upper portion. The female flowers are green bud-like structures, always placed near the stalk's base. Both male and female flowers have nectaries, and pollination is effected largely by insects seeking nectar, though some pollen is windborne. The fertilized female flowers ripen quickly through late summer, to mature as chestnuts by October. These glossy, deep-brown nuts are grouped in threes, though often only one actually ripens. They lie within a thick, green, leathery husk bearing yellow spines. This husk, which gives little protection against hungry animals, usually splits when the falling nuts strike the ground. Most nuts are eaten by squirrels, mice, pigeons, pheasants and other creatures, including man. The survivors sprout next spring; keeping their seed-leaves within the shell, they send up a sturdy shoot bearing normal foliage.

People cook and eat the delicious chestnuts in various ways – roasted, boiled for stuffing turkeys, or steeped in sugar as *marrons glacés*. Most are imported.

Sweet chestnut bark is pale brownish grey, and becomes deeply ribbed in a net-mesh pattern, usually with a spiral trend. The timber beneath has a remarkably narrow, pale-brown, outer sapwood zone. The central heartwood is rich golden-brown, very strong, and naturally very durable. Because it often develops splits, called 'shakes', sweet chestnut wood is rarely used as large

planks though it serves well for smaller timbers. Chestnut poles are exceptionally valuable, because their large heartwood content ensures long service, and also because they are easily split into triangular pales. The familiar cleft chestnut paling, made by stringing pales on galvanized wire, comes mainly from coppices in Kent. After the poles have been cut, a fresh crop springs up from stumps, giving successive harvests every fifteen years.

Though height growth is moderate, not exceeding 35 m (114 ft), exceptional chestnuts become our oldest and stoutest trees. One at Canford, Dorset, is 13 m (43 ft) round and possibly 500 years old.

The smooth-barked grey trunk of beech rises from a buttressed base.

BEECH

Fagus sylvatica   FAGACEAE

Beech is native only to the southern half of Britain, including South Wales, but it has been introduced and
planted on woodland estates throughout Scotland, Ireland
and northern England as well. It may be known at once
by its smooth metallic-grey bark, which keeps its texture
and colour no matter how old the tree may grow. Seldom

exceeding 200 years in age, beech grows to a great size, up to 43 m (142 ft) tall and 8 m (26 ft) round.

The slender, rather zigzag twigs of beech carry distinctive winter buds, always alternately set. Long, narrow, and clad in dry brown scales, they taper to a sharp point. In April they release tender, bright pale-green leaves, which have an oval outline, a wavy edge, a short stalk and a pointed tip. These leaves darken and get firmer as summer advances, to turn orange-brown before falling in October. On young trees and beeches clipped as hedges, faded fawn-brown leaves persist all winter through. Copper beech is a foliage colour variety, usually *purpurea*.

The male catkins of beech open in April, too, in groups on young twigs. Each catkin has a long stalk and consists of a tassel of about fifteen flowers. Each separate male flower has a hairy, four-lobed green calyx and about eight yellow stamens.

The female catkins are short green bud-like structures, almost stalkless, and set close against twigs. Each has an oval green cupule holding two very small flowers. Each flower consists of a four-lobed green calyx and a pistil bearing three stigmas. During the summer the cupule becomes hard and woody and develops soft brown spines on its outer surfaces. In October the husk turns brown and splits to release the seeds within. There may be one or two seeds — the beech nuts; often only one develops, or in bad years none at all. The beech nut is triangular in shape, with a hard, smooth, brown shell and a firm white kernel within. Squirrels, wood pigeons, and many other sorts of bird and beast eat beech nuts greedily, so helping to spread them. In the past they were valued as 'mast' for feeding swine, though the variable annual seed crop made them an unreliable aid towards fat pork.

After passing the winter on the damp leaf mould of the forest floor, a beech nut starts life in spring by splitting its shell, sending down a root, and expanding two broad,

fleshy, bright green seed-leaves. Normal foliage follows.

Beech timber is a uniform pale-fawn colour, with no obvious features except for tiny red-brown specks of ray tissue, present everywhere. It is widely used for kitchen furniture, school desks and everyday chairs, where strength counts for more than appearance. Beech works evenly to a smooth surface in any direction, and is used for mallet heads, small tool handles, carpenters' planes, and other handy wooden objects – always indoors, because it is not durable when exposed to the weather.

CRACK WILLOW

Salix fragilis   SALICACEAE

The crack willow takes its name from a remarkable
character of its twigs. If you pull one back with a sharp
tug, it will break away from its larger stem with a distinctly audible 'crack!' Nobody is sure why this tree grows
such brittle twigs, but the property does aid its spread.
It grows along watersides, and twigs, torn off by gusty
winds, get carried downstream and strike root when

stranded on damp mud-banks. The brittle property extends to the wood which is, in consequence, rarely used.

Crack willow is, in other respects, a typical member of the willow genus, *Salix*. All the willows are easily identified as such, during most of the year, by a peculiar feature of their buds. These are *oval* and enclosed within a *single* smooth external scale; except in seedlings they are always set singly along the twigs. Though all willows have simple leaves, their shape varies markedly from round through oval to long, narrow, lance-shaped leaves. Crack willow has this last-named form, and its leaves are uniform pale green, not shining as in the otherwise similar white willow.

With rare exceptions, all willows bear either male *or* female catkins. Very occasionally you may find 'male' and 'female' branches on the same tree. The sex of each tree or branch remains constant if a cutting is grown from it. On most willows, catkins open in March, before the leaves expand, providing one of the gayest sights of spring. They are often gathered for indoor decoration, as 'palm blossom', from a traditional link with the palms used at Eastertide in the Holy Land. Both male and female catkins are oval structures clad in a mass of soft, white, silky hairs, which have earned these trees the nick-name of 'pussy willows'. The curious word 'catkin', which experts agree can only mean 'little cat', was apparently first applied to the soft, furry, oval flower clusters of willow. It is now used, by analogy, to cover a wide range of flower structures on other trees, often very different in appearance.

The pollination of willows is effected in part by wind, and in part by insects. The male flowers are adapted to scatter, and the female flowers to receive, wind-borne pollen grains. But flowers of both sexes also have nectaries, and are visited eagerly by hungry bees in early spring, when few other blossoms are open. Each separate male flower consists of a hairy bract, a nectary, and two

116

This huge crack willow bole, beside a stream, bears typically ragged grey bark, with a meshwork of broken ribs.

golden anthers that scatter pollen. Overall, male catkins show a gay yellow shade.

Each female flower has again a hairy bract and a nectary, with a long oval pistil ending in two stigmas. The dominant colour of female catkins is a silvery greenish grey.

Following pollination, the female pistils develop rapidly, and are ripe by midsummer. They then split lengthwise and release a large number of tiny seeds, each bearing a tuft of white hairs to aid its dispersal by the wind.

Each seed must sprout within a few weeks of ripening, or else perish. This explains why willows can only colonize new surfaces of bare soil, as on banks of streams or sand-pits, and are seldom found invading grassy fields. A minute proportion alight on damp earth or mud, germinate successfully, and survive. The little seedling raises first two seed-leaves, then two small opposite leaves, and next a pair of larger opposite leaves. Typical solitary leaves then follow.

The wood of willows is a pale creamy-brown colour, with pinkish-brown heartwood. It has an open, rather woolly texture, and holds in the living tree a great deal of water. When seasoned it becomes exceptionally light in weight, making a poor fire-wood. It is perishable out of doors and has only the specialized uses described later under white willow and osier.

The bark of crack willow is at first smooth, and orange-brown on young twigs. Later it develops a network of shallow ribs, and becomes grey. Crack willow is never a large tree, and often develops an irregular, bushy form due to frequent branch breakages. Maximum height is 15 m (50 ft) and greatest girth 1.5 m (5 ft).

WHITE WILLOW

Salix alba SALICACEAE

White willow is easily known by the silvery appearance of its leaves, which are clad in white down on their undersides. This bright colour is strikingly revealed when wind stirs the foliage. The upper surface of each leaf is pale green. In outline the leaves are narrowly oval, or lanceolate, with pointed tips and shallow-toothed edges.

The flowering pattern follows that previously described for crack willows, but white willow is a more handsome

119

White willow's grey bark has a regular pattern of ribs and fissures; boles are often divided and tortuous.

and better-shaped tree. It can reach 25 m (81 ft) in height, with a girth of 3.4 m (11 ft). Its timber is more supple and hence more highly valued. The bark is smooth and grey on young twigs, but develops a deeply furrowed network of ribs and hollows on tree trunks as they grow stouter.

Most of the pollard willows which grow beside the streams of the Midlands and southern England belong to this species. These stunted trees were formerly lopped every two years or so by farmers, who obtained thin stems suitable for plaiting into hurdles, or repairing gaps in hedges. Another characteristic willow form is weeping willow, in which branches droop downwards towards water which gives the foliage reflected sunlight. Most weeping willows are *Salix alba* variety *tristis*.

Timber from good stems of white willow is soft, light and easily carved or turned. It was long used for making household and dairy utensils such as bowls and plates, for yokes worn by dairymaids when carrying buckets of milk suspended from their shoulders, and the light 'trugs' or wooden baskets still made by hand in Sussex.

The best-known use of willow wood, however, is for making cricket bats. The strain of trees preferred is the cricket bat willow, *Salix alba* variety *coerulea*, a variety of the white willow distinguished by its shapely form, with a conical, tapering crown. In practice it is always female, and is increased by cuttings. Its foliage has a pleasing bluish-green shade. Cricket bat willows are grown on rich farm meadowlands, and spaced 9 m (30 ft) apart. The lowest 3 m (10 ft) of stem is always pruned, so that no knots can mar the timber. Twelve years after planting, the trees are usually stout enough for felling. The valuable butt length, 2.4 m (8 ft) long, is cut off, and then cleft by hand into wedge-shaped segments. After careful seasoning, which ensures even shrinkage, three bat lengths are cut from each segment, and then shaped by hand to make bat blades — very light, tough and not liable to warp or split in the course of play.

GOAT WILLOW

Salix caprea SALICACEAE

The goat willow is so named because its early spring foliage is a favourite food of tame goats. It is also called the 'common sallow', or in Scotland, the 'saugh'. You can find it everywhere about the countryside, usually on the edges of ponds or patches of waste land, quarry banks, and the ruins of abandoned buildings. Its leaves are oval, dull green above and paler below, with prominent veins. Their shape distinguishes them from the 'timber' willows, the white and the crack, and from the osiers described later. But there are many sorts of sallow, or wild bush willow, and close botanical study is needed to determine each species exactly.

Goat willow never grows taller than a large bush, up to 6.7 m (22 ft) high, and its trunk is rarely over half a metre ($1\frac{1}{2}$ ft) round. The bark remains smooth, and dark greenish grey. Stems are too small to yield commercial timber, though gypsies have long used goat willow for whittling into hand-made clothes-pegs, once on sale in every country market.

This exceptionally large goat willow trunk shows typical, random, shallow fissures; pale grey.

Goat willow is mainly valued as a source of 'palm blossom' and of honey for the bees. Because it grows so freely on stream banks and river shingle, it probably plays a significant part in fixing loose gravel and mud, so holding the streams to their courses and checking soil erosion. It also hides the scars of industry.

Smooth-barked grey-green osier willow stems spread out from a low stool.

OSIER WILLOWS

Salix viminalis   SALICACEAE
S. purpurea

Osiers – a name linked to French *osier* and introduced by
the Normans – are a large group of cultivated willows
having supple stems exceptionally suitable for basket-
making. Their older English name is withes or withies.
The common osier, *Salix viminalis*, which bears long,
slender, lance-shaped leaves forms, as a wild tree, a low
straggling bush. The purple osier, *S. purpurea*, has purple
stems, slender catkins, and leaves set in opposite pairs; it
is always shrub-like in growth.

For basket work, osiers are always grown from cuttings,
which are planted about 60 cm (2 ft) apart on rich agri-
cultural land in well-watered lowlands. The first year's
growth is cut back and rejected, and the rooted cutting
then forms a 'stool' which will send up clusters of fresh
shoots for many years to come. Each autumn the crop
of one-year-old shoots, which often exceed 2 m (6 ft) in
length, is harvested with a sharp curved knife. These
shoots, now termed 'rods' or 'wands', are very light,
tough, and supple. Provided they are handled whilst
moist, they can readily be bent into the intricate shapes
needed for a hand-woven wooden basket.

Sometimes they are used with their natural brown
bark intact. More usually it is stripped off by simple
machinery to expose the white wood. If the rods are
boiled before stripping, natural dyes in the bark stain the
wood bright buff – a typical basket colour. For fine
work, the round stems are split, by hand, into thin narrow
bands.

Formerly basket weaving was a widespread cottage
industry, for baskets were needed everywhere for market-
ing fruit, vegetables, or fish, and for packaging food,
laundry, and many other kinds of goods. Osiers were

also used for making fish-traps, lobster-pots and even bird-cages. In many marshy valleys you may still find abandoned osier beds. But the only place in England where commercial cultivation continues is Sedgemoor, near the town of Langport in Somerset. Most of the osiers that basket-makers use nowadays are imported, mainly from Argentina.

POPLARS: ASPEN

Populus tremula Salicaceae

The names 'poplar' and '*Populus*' are distantly derived from the ancient Greek root word *papaillo* meaning to flutter, which is linked to the French word *papillon* for a butterfly. Poplars are so named because their leaves are set on long flexible stalks, with an odd twist, so that they move in the slightest breeze. Poplars can often be picked out in summer because their leaves quiver when those of other trees are still. This constant motion aids the poplar's growth, because it increases the intake of air by the leaves, and hence the rate of carbon fixation from the air's carbon dioxide. But it also means that the leaves transpire water rapidly, just as a wet handkerchief waved in the wind dries quickly. Poplars are therefore 'thirsty' trees. They thrive best beside rivers or in marshy places where ample water is available in summer. Aspen in particular is a tree of the swamps.

To cope with the rapid flow of sap from the roots to their shaking leaves, poplars develop a distinctive timber. It has exceptionally large thin-walled cells and pores. This

The smooth grey bark of aspen poplar bears characteristic diamond-shaped hollows.

means that, although it is heavy when alive and full of sap, it becomes exceptionally light when dry, and therefore has little value as fire-wood. It has no great strength and decays in a few years if used out of doors. In colour it is pale yellow or creamy brown with no clear distinction of heartwood.

Such an odd timber might appear to have no practical use, but in fact poplar is highly valued because, when cut into thin sheets, it proves lighter, tougher and more flexible than any other wood. These sheets, called rotary-cut veneers, are obtained by turning a whole poplar log round against a long sharp knife fixed in a powerful lathe, like a giant pencil-sharpener. Veneers are used for making match-sticks, which are sliced from them by high-speed machines, and also for match-boxes and the 'chip' baskets used, especially in southern Europe, for packaging vegetables, fruit and cheese. Much of our fresh food reaches the shops in these white, thin, poplar wood baskets.

The winter buds of poplars, set singly along the twigs, are many-scaled and pointed, but have no simple feature that might help you to say, 'This must be a poplar.' The leaves, however, have a distinctive character in that their veins run through their broad blades in a *random*, irregular fashion not found on other trees. In outline the leaves vary from round or oval, through triangular, to diamond shaped. Most poplars have 'simple', unlobed leaves, but on vigorous shoots of white or grey poplars distinct lobes develop. Aspen leaves are round, with an indented edge. Their long stalks are flattened sideways, which leaves them free to flutter in all but dead-still air.

Every poplar tree is either wholly male or wholly female. Most kinds are easily propagated by cuttings, which keep the sex, as well as all the other characters, of the parent tree. Aspen is an exception in that it can, in practice, only be raised from seed or from sucker shoots springing up from its spreading roots.

Poplar catkins open in March before the leaves have expanded. This enables their wind-borne pollen to float on the wind unhindered by foliage. The male catkins, which look like long, furry, red-and-yellow caterpillars, consist of a hanging main stalk bearing numerous individual flowers. Each flower is made up of a large bract and a group of about thirty stamens with large, crimson anthers that shed golden pollen. Soon after ripening these male catkins fade and fall.

Female poplar catkins also consist of a central, drooping stalk, bearing a string of separate flowers, but the whole structure has a general resemblance to a string of beads or a necklace. Each separate flower has a green bract and a single pistil, topped by a stigma to catch wind-borne pollen. After fertilization, the pistil ripens rapidly to become, by May, a greenish-brown woody capsule, holding numerous seeds, each tipped with a tuft of white hairs. The capsule then splits to release them, and they drift away on the wind. This white, hairy poplar seed, which blows everywhere, is unpopular with gardeners because it makes paths and lawns look untidy; and also with householders since it drifts indoors or sticks to wet paint. In consequence, very few nurserymen stock or sell female poplars. In fact a female poplar of any kind is something of a 'find' in the countryside today.

The little seeds that drift away only retain the power of life for a few short weeks. In that time they must alight on damp soil or else perish, as the vast majority do. A successful seedling sends up two plump oval seed-leaves, forming a facing pair; these are followed by normal foliage with solitary leaves.

On good land poplars grow faster than any other trees, sometimes achieving 2 m (6 ft) of height growth in one year. They can reach immense size, up to 43 m (140 ft) tall and 8.2 m (27 ft) round in Britain, and even larger elsewhere. But they are not long-lived trees, and seldom stand for more than 100 years. Many poplars have an irregular branching habit and can be picked out at a distance, in winter, because they look more like a 'branch stuck in the ground' than a properly balanced tree.

Bark characters vary markedly, from smooth white surfaces in white poplar to deeply fissured grey bark in the so-called black kinds.

Poplars are commonly grown from cuttings, and so all the trees in one plantation or avenue are likely to have the same parent tree. They are then said to belong to the same 'clone' and naturally look very much alike.

White poplar

Since poplars transpire water rapidly from the soil in summer, they intensify the uneven shrinkage that occurs on clay soils. It is unsafe, therefore, to plant them near buildings in such places, for this root action can disturb otherwise sound foundations.

White poplar bark, initially white and smooth, develops a pale-grey, round-ribbed pattern later.

WHITE POPLAR

Populus alba   SALICACEAE

This handsome tree, illustrated on page 131, is probably native to England, as it is to most of western Europe. But it is rare, as the eastern fens that were once its home have been cleared and drained, and it is only occasionally planted. It is most likely to be found colonizing landslips or sea-cliffs with moist clay soils. It resists salty sea winds and is planted for shelter along the coast.

Its bark is greenish white to pale grey, and smooth except at the base of old trees, where it may become rough and black. The young shoots and buds are clad in white down. The underside of each leaf is also white and downy, but the upper surface is smooth and dark green. Leaves turn an attractive golden shade in autumn, but the whiteness of the undersides persists even after they fall. Leaf shape is very variable, even on the same tree. Leaves on vigorous shoots are large and clearly five-lobed, while at the other extreme those on slow-growing side shoots are small and almost round.

Large white poplars are rare, for most trees grow in crowded natural groves springing up as sucker shoots. As an isolated park specimen, however, it may reach 24 m (80 ft) tall and 5 m (17 ft) round.

Grey poplar

GREY POPLAR

Populus canescens   SALICACEAE

The status of this handsome and wind-tolerant tree still
puzzles botanists. It may be either a hybrid, or else
an intermediate form, between the aspen and the white
poplar. But all the same it is called a species, *Populus
canescens*, in most text-books. It is apparently native to
England, but is rarely found truly wild. Gardeners nearly

134

Lombardy poplar

always plant the male tree, which bears attractive crimson spring catkins. Female trees are rare, so it can seldom spread by seed. In cultivation it is increased by sucker shoots.

The characters of grey poplar lie midway between those of aspen and white poplar. Its bark is smooth and grey rather than white. Young shoots and the undersides of leaves are white at first, but as summer advances these leaf surfaces become smooth and pale green. The leaves

Grey poplar forms dark rugged ribs on old trunks.

vary in shape, from round to diamond form, or even shallowly lobed.

Grey poplar is usually a vigorous tree, and can reach 34 m (110 ft) tall and 5.8 m (19 ft) round.

BLACK AND LOMBARDY POPLARS

Populus nigra and variety *italica* SALICACEAE

The typical, normally-branching form of black poplar, *Populus nigra*, occurs wild over most of Europe, including the English lowlands from Lancashire south-east to Essex. It forms a spreading, much-branched tree with a thick, rough-surfaced and deeply fissured grey bark. Its trunk shows characteristic swellings. The twigs are strongly ribbed, angular and somewhat zigzag, and the brown, pointed buds have prominent scales. The long-stalked leaves are diamond shaped to oval, with toothed edges and a blunt-pointed tip.

Though black poplar grows readily from cuttings it

Lombardy poplar has a rough, strongly fluted trunk with a buttressed base; brownish grey.

does not produce sucker shoots. Wild trees arise only from wind-borne seed, and it has become rare because modern farming leaves little lowland free for fresh colonization. It can grow fast and tall, up to 34 m (110 ft), and become a wide-girthed tree, up to 6 m (20 ft) round.

To many people the name 'poplar' means a tree with the slender outline of the Lombardy kind, as illustrated on page 135. In this remarkable form all the branches point upwards in the same direction as the main stem, which they follow closely. Such trees are called 'fastigiate', meaning 'shaped like a sweeping broom'. Lombardy poplar was first discovered on the plains of northern Italy.

Black poplar

It is easily increased by cuttings and has now been planted in all the temperate countries of the world for its unique landscape value. It also provides, quickly, a narrow screen to shelter crops from wind or hide an ugly factory.

Lombardy poplars, which have the botanical name of *Populus nigra* variety *italica*, are usually male trees, though females are also known. Despite its slender form, it is rarely exceptionally tall; the tallest one only reaches 35 m (115 ft), while the stoutest is 4.6 m (15 ft) round. The countless branches all leave knots in the wood, and there are numerous ribs on the rough, grey-barked trunk, so the Lombardy poplar is worthless as timber.

Balsam poplar

139

Foresters growing poplars for timber today plant *hybrid* black poplars in preference to the native species. These hybrids have been bred by crossing various wild poplars. One of the commonest and most successful is the cultivar *Populus* 'Serotina' obtained by crossing the European black poplar with an American species, *P. deltoides*; it is also called the 'black Italian' poplar. The selected hybrids, which are always increased by cuttings, have been chosen for good form, rapid and vigorous growth, light branching habit, and resistance to disease. You will find them standing in plantations along marshy valleys, evenly spaced

Black poplar bears thick, irregular, pale-grey bark ribs.

Balsam poplars have thin grey bark which flakes off old stems.

about 6 m (20 ft) apart, each looking exactly like its neighbour. The lower section of each straight trunk is always pruned clear of branches, as the knots that these form would make the logs unsuitable for match and basket veneers.

Hybrid poplars grow very fast, increasing by up to 2 m (6 ft) each year. Plantations often attain timber size, ready for felling, only thirty years after planting. Individual trees in parks grow very tall, up to 43 m (140 ft), and stout, up to 8.2 m (27 ft) round.

141

BALSAM POPLAR

Populus trichocarpa SALICACEAE

The picture on page 139 shows a typical poplar of the balsam group, most of which are native to North America. This particular species, *Populus trichocarpa*, comes from the Pacific coastal region, where it is called the 'black cottonwood' – from its hairy seeds – or the 'western balsam poplar'. In spring, just as the leaves unfold, it fills the air with the delightful fragrance of the sticky gum or 'balsam' that protects its buds from insect or fungal attack. The leaves are, at that time, a vividly bright yellowish green, and sticky with the fragrant resin that pervades all the tree's soft tissues. Later their upper surface becomes a deep, shiny green, with grey-green undersides showing a meshwork of greenish-yellow veins. In outline they are slender ovoid structures, midway between a diamond shape and an oval. The bark, olive grey on young twigs, becomes brownish grey on larger ones, and eventually very thick and deeply fissured. For illustration of bole, see page 141.

In America the balsam poplars yield valued timbers and attain great size along the riversides where they thrive. They may reach 68 m (225 ft) tall, with girths of 7.6 m (25 ft). In Europe, up till now, they have been planted mainly for their attractive foliage and fragrance, though certain hybrids hold promise as rapid timber producers. Another hybrid, the Ontario balsam poplar, *P.* × *gileadensis*, also called *Populus candicans*, has been widely planted on industrial waste land, because it forms thickets from its vigorous suckers, where few other trees can survive.

CONIFERS

The name 'conifer' implies a tree that bears cones, and the common feature of nearly all trees in this group are their woody cones, each made up of tough brown scales carrying one or, more usually, two seeds. Cones develop from small female flowers that have received wind-borne pollen from male flowers. The yellow male flower-clusters of many conifers are obvious to the eye in spring, but they fade quickly. Few people notice the little female flowers until they have developed into cones, which may take a few months or two or three years, depending on the kind of tree. Every conifer has a distinctive cone form, and since most cones persist for a year or more this aids identification.

Conifers are also called 'coniferous trees' or 'needle-leaved trees' from the shape of their characteristic foliage, or 'softwoods' because the timber of most kinds is softer and more easily worked than the 'hardwood' of broad-leaved trees. They are sometimes known as 'evergreens' since most kinds retain their leaves through the winter. Botanists call them 'gymnosperms' meaning 'naked-seeded trees', because their embryo seed, the ovule, develops unprotected on the surface of each cone scale; though later on it becomes, in most kinds, very firmly shut up in the hard ripening cone. But eventually, in dry weather, the cone scales open and the seeds flutter out. Watch for this on a dry autumn day in a larch wood, or a late spring day in a pine wood. Each seed bears a papery brown wing that aids its spread.

Conifers are being widely planted today in many countries because they grow faster on poorer soils and under colder or sometimes drier climates than most broad-leaved trees. The timber they yield so quickly is both readily worked and strong enough for most uses, such as building. It is also lighter in weight and more consistent in character than most broadleaved timbers or 'hardwoods'. Its long fibres fit it well for paper, cardboard, chipboard and similar man-made materials which we draw from the forests in ever-growing amounts. But many conifers are grown simply for ornament, or to give year-round shelter to gardens or fields.

The simple foliage patterns of conifers present a real problem of identification until you know the clues, then it becomes easy. Another difficulty is the careless use, by most people who are not foresters, gardeners or botanists, of words like 'fir', 'spruce' or 'cedar'. Each can only fit a particular small group of trees. The key below will enable you to name common woodland conifers, though not all the rarities found in some parks or large gardens.

Fern-like foliage
Two common conifers, especially frequent in gardens, bear leaves in fronds rather like ferns. The separate needles overlap, hiding the twigs and buds completely. Lawson cypress has thin foliage, and tiny buds that you cannot feel through the leaves; cones, if present, are round woody knobs. Western red cedar has more fleshy foliage, and if you feel the leaves you can sense the shape of hidden buds; its cones are slender papery ovals.

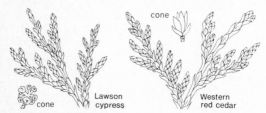

Lawson cypress
cone
cone
Western red cedar

Needles in twos, threes or clusters
Scots pine and many related pines bear long needles two-by-two, arising from tiny 'short shoots' hidden in papery bracts. (In some rarer pines, not described further here,

144

needles are grouped in
fives or threes.) Cones
are oval with hard
woody scales.

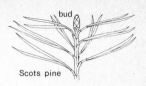

Scots pine

Juniper, a native shrub, bears stiff, spiky needles in threes
projecting all round its twigs; it ripens blue-black berries.
Western hemlock, a graceful timber tree, carries three
ranks of soft needles down its twigs. The variable lengths
of these ranks enable you to name it on sight. Cones are
small, and oval, with papery scales.

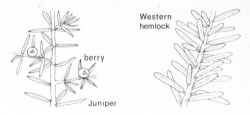

Western
hemlock

berry

Juniper

If numerous needles, soft in texture, are grouped round
woody knobs, the foliage is that of a larch. Larch needles
fall in winter, but the woody knobs still make identification easy. Note, however, that larches always have solitary
needles at branch tips; their cones are barrel shaped,
often with 'hollow' ends.

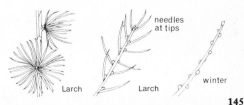

needles
at tips

Larch   Larch   winter

Solitary needles

Look first for a little 'peg' at the base of each needle. If it is present and you pull a green needle, this peg tears away. It indicates a spruce, a very widely planted tree. When spruce needles fade naturally, the woody pegs remain, leaving typically rough twigs. Spruce cones are cylindrical and droop downwards.

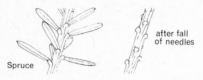

after fall
of needles

Spruce

If there are no pegs, pull a needle off to check that it leaves a *circular scar*. This indicates a yew, which has a *leafy* bud, or a Douglas fir, which has a *pointed brown* bud, or one of the silver firs, with *short blunt buds*, often resinous.

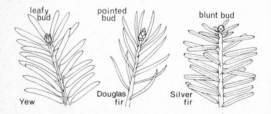

leafy
bud

pointed
bud

blunt bud

Yew

Douglas
fir

Silver
fir

Yew needles have no resinous scent, the others are fragrant. The fruit of yew is a red berry, with a hard black seed. Douglas fir carries a very distinctive cone, with a three-pointed bract below each scale. The silver firs, which form the *Abies* genus, and include grand fir and noble fir, bear large upright cones, though these fall early in autumn.

YEW

Taxus baccata   TAXACEAE

The dark, mysterious evergreen yew is native throughout
most of Europe and the British Isles. It forms natural
groves in most ancient forests, particularly the New
Forest and the Forest of Dean. It thrives on chalk, with
a notable wood at Kingley Vale near Chichester in
Sussex, and others on Box Hill in Surrey. Yew's association with churchyards dates from the first Christian
missionaries, who preached the gospel below the year-
round shelter of this spreading evergreen tree, symbol of
everlasting life. The oldest churchyard yews, with ages

estimated at 1500 years, and the stoutest measuring 10.7 m (35 ft), are certainly older than the churches themselves. Exceptionally, in woodlands yews grow as tall as 27 m (90 ft).

Yew is easily known by its needle-shaped leaves, set in two ranks along fine twigs ending in small leafy buds. They are very dark green above, paler below, and fall after several years' life, fading to brown. They cast deep shade, and no green plants grow on the shaded ground below. They are poisonous to cattle and other farm live-

Yew boles, often fluted, bear thin reddish-brown, flaky-surfaced, fibrous bark.

stock, especially when clipped and half-withered, yet animals often browse around yews, suffering no harm. The bark is thin, smooth and reddish brown, and flakes away gradually; it is poisonous too. Both trunk and branches are usually deeply fluted and fissured, and rarely truly round. Irish yew is an upright form, variety *fastigiata*.

Every yew tree is either male or female. Male trees bear pretty clusters of yellow stamens amid their foliage in February, shedding abundant golden pollen. Female flowers, green and bud-like at first, expand by the next autumn into distinctive fruits. Each consists of a hard, greenish-black seed, which is very poisonous, set within a cup of pink flesh, which is harmless though sickly-sweet to the taste. Birds, especially thrushes and fieldfares, pluck the fruits for this nutritious pulp, and either scatter the seed or swallow it, later voiding it unharmed. It lies on the ground for about eighteen months before sprouting as a seedling with two opposite, tender, pale-green seed-leaves, which last through only one summer. Normal evergreen foliage follows.

Yew timber has a very distinctive heartwood, rusty-red brown in colour with a purplish tinge; it is dense, strong, and naturally very durable. The dead-white sapwood layer around it is very thin, rarely over 2 cm (0.8 in.) thick. Because of the irregular outline of the trunk, it is only used for decorative work, as in high-grade furniture, chairs and tables, trays, bowls and wood sculpture. Coarse logs make lasting fence posts, or good fire-wood. Selected straight staves, cut from large trunks, provide long bows for archers, for yew has greater elasticity and strength than any other timber.

GRAND FIR

Abies grandis P<small>INACEAE</small>

This lovely conifer originates on the Pacific seaboard of
Canada and the United States, where it forms stately
groves of tall timber. It was introduced to Britain in

1831 and is now widely planted, often as a decorative tree, but also for its high yields of timber. It will tolerate shade so foresters use it to fill gaps in woodlands, or to 'underplant' sparse crops of a lower-yielding species, such as larch, in order to increase the yield from the land as a whole.

Grand fir is best known by the very regular arrangement of its long, deep-green needles on each side of its twigs, in herring-bone fashion. Actually they are placed spirally around the twig, but twists in their short basal stalks bring them into two ranks. The buds at the twig tips are blunt (not pointed as in Douglas fir) and resinous. If you pull off a single needle it leaves a flat circular scar (not a peg as in spruce). On upright leading shoots the needles stand out all round the stem.

Male flowers of grand fir open in May, as clusters of yellow stamens, set in groups on the leafy twigs; the stamens scatter wind-borne pollen. The female flowers appear at the same time, as small upright green bud-like structures. After pollinating they expand rapidly. By September they have enlarged to barrel-shaped cones that stand upright (never drooping as in spruce). They ripen quickly, turning pale brown, but within a few early autumn weeks they shatter. The brown scales fall away, releasing two seeds from below each scale, and all that remains is the erect central mid-rib.

Grand fir seeds are brown and triangular-oval in shape, and each is attached to a triangular, papery, brown wing that aids wind dispersal. Seedlings have a curious seed-leaf pattern, with about ten short leaves alternating with as many long ones. The first true needles stand out all round the upright shoot, and the flat herring-bone arrangement only appears when side shoots develop.

Grand fir has a remarkably smooth grey bark, which often develops swellings called resin blisters. Prick one and the fragrant sticky resin, a protection against insect attack, quickly oozes out. The timber is creamy white to very pale brown, with no colour distinction of heartwood. It works easily and is moderately strong. Though not naturally durable, and unsuited to outdoor use, it is a good material for joinery and packaging, and yields excellent paper pulp.

Grand fir is, with us, the most vigorous of the silver fir genus, *Abies*. It can grow in Britain to 55 m (181 ft) tall and up to 6 m (20 ft) round. It is closely related to noble fir, described later, to the European silver fir (*A. alba*) of the Alps, and the balsam fir (*A. balsamea*) of eastern North America.

Grand fir, smooth at first, develops shallow, irregular grey plates.

Noble fir's stout bole always bears smooth grey bark, with occasional fissures.

NOBLE FIR

Abies procera   PINACEAE

The valleys of the Rocky Mountains, from the State of Washington south to California, are the homeland of this beautiful silver fir. It is now widely planted, mainly as a decorative tree, in parks and on woodland fringes throughout the British Isles. The people of Denmark have adopted this American immigrant as their national Christmas tree, and its elegant foliage is widely used by florists everywhere for decorative arrangements.

Noble fir, so named for its handsome appearance, is easily recognized by its upswept foliage. The needles on both side of its twigs bend forwards and upwards to form a thick mat on the upper side, facing the light. Their colour is a shimmering silver grey, tending towards bluish green where they become shaded. Both their

colour, which is due to a surface water-retaining wax, and their arrangement are devices to lessen water loss under bright sunshine in an arid climate. The buds at twig tips are blunt, and grey with resin, a protection against insect attack.

The male flowers of noble fir are clusters of yellow stamens, scattering golden pollen; they open amid the foliage in May. The female flowers open at the same time as green bud-like structures. They expand, after pollination by wind, to become huge upright cones. Green at first, they ripen and turn brown in September. These attractive cones, up to 25 cm (10 in.) long and 5 cm (2 in.) thick, show a very clear double spiral pattern of woody scales. Below each scale stands a brown bract with a reflexed, three-pointed tip; this unmistakable feature has earned the tree its second name of 'feathercone fir'. Unfortunately the cones are short-lived. They shatter within a few weeks of ripening, releasing two seeds from beneath each scale. These oval-triangular, grey-brown seeds have triangular wings to aid spread by wind. Seedlings have a first whorl of seed-leaves, alternating in two different lengths, then straight early needles; the upswept pattern first shows on side branches.

Noble fir has a smooth grey bark, which scarcely roughens with age. It often bears conspicuous resin blisters, holding sticky resin, which checks invading insects and seals off wounds from fungal spores. The trunks of large trees show a very marked degree of taper, possibly linked to the need to withstand exposure and wind force with a relatively weak wood. Noble fir timber, which is pale cream in colour and shows no obvious heartwood, has only moderate strength, though it can be used for the same purposes as grand fir wood.

Slow-growing at first, noble fir speeds up later and tall trees withstand fierce sea winds near Scotland's west coast. The tallest tree recorded in Britain reaches 46 m (150 ft); and the stoutest is 5 m (16 ft) round.

DOUGLAS FIR

Pseudotsuga menziesii   PINACEAE

One of the world's tallest trees, the Douglas fir comes from Oregon and British Columbia, where it was discovered by the Scottish botanist Archibald Menzies in 1791, as recorded by its scientific name. Later, in 1827, another Scotsman, David Douglas, sent seed to Europe, where it has been widely planted as a timber producer ever since. A Douglas fir felled on Vancouver Island in 1895 scaled 127 m (417 ft), an all-time record for any tree. Though only known in Britain for 150 years, Douglas fir provides our tallest specimen trees. There is one 55 m (181 ft) tall at Powis Castle in Wales and another 53 m (175 ft) high at The Hermitage, Dunkeld, Scotland. The greatest recorded British girth is 7.3 m (24 ft).

The sweet-scented resinous foliage of Douglas fir resembles that of silver firs. The two-ranked needles are dark green above, and paler beneath, and there is no peg at their base. The buds, which readily distinguish it, are slender and pointed, with chestnut-brown scales, resembling those of beech. Male flowers are borne in clusters on young branches in May and are loaded with golden pollen. The female flowers are green, egg-shaped structures which expand rapidly after wind pollination, turning brown in autumn. As they grow they develop below each cone scale a remarkable straight bract with three points, the central one being longer than its neighbours. Combined with an oval cone that always *hangs downwards*, these bracts provide a certain key feature for identification. Their only parallel is found in noble fir, but that tree bears cylindrical cones that stand upright, and its bracts are reflexed.

The cone scales open in spring and scatter small winged seeds, two from beneath each scale. Seedlings first open a whorl of about twenty seed-leaves and then bear normal foliage of solitary needles around the shoot.

Douglas fir yields a remarkably strong timber. No matter how fast or slowly it grows it always forms a clear band of hard red-brown summerwood in each annual ring. Hence its general character and appearance resembles pine timber and it is marketed as 'Oregon pine' or 'British Columbian pine'. It is used for building and heavy constructional work; it also yields a strong plywood with a bold pattern of colour and texture.

Douglas fir bark is at first smooth and dark grey. As

Douglas fir develops exceptionally rugged, stoutly ribbed bark, greyish chocolate-brown with pale orange-grey channels.

the tree trunk expands, irregular fissures appear running more or less vertically. The islands of bark between these soon grow very thick, and various shades of light brown become apparent between them. This thick, rough, irregular mottled brown bark makes recognition of mature trees easy.

WESTERN HEMLOCK

Tsuga heterophylla   PINACEAE

This graceful evergreen conifer is immediately known by
the varying lengths of its needles. These appear to be
scattered along the twigs in a random fashion, though
there are in fact three series, of three different lengths,
set in a spiral. Another unusual feature is the drooping
leading shoot, possibly a device to shed winter snow.

However, the hemlock grows steadily upwards, even though its main bud points downwards!

This species is called 'western' because it comes from the west coast of North America. The climate there matches that of western Europe, and western hemlock is being planted on a growing scale in Britain because it quickly yields heavy crops of reasonably strong, pale-brown timber. The alternative species, eastern hemlock, *Tsuga canadensis*, does not thrive so well in Europe.

Each individual needle of hemlock stands on a short stalk, with a 'cushion' but no obvious peg at its base. It is silvery green below and darker above. The buds are short and blunt. Male flowers develop abundantly in May, in clusters amid the foliage, and shed golden pollen. The small female flowers appear as green, bud-shaped structures, grouped near branch tips. They ripen to bright brown cones about 2.5 cm (1 in.) long, with short scales, which make a decorative display on the dark branches in autumn. Each tiny, oval, brown seed is wind-borne on a triangular wing. When it sprouts next spring it opens exactly three seed-leaves, a rare feature. Normal foliage, with needles of varied lengths, follow.

Hemlock bears a black bark, with shallow fissures, which has long been used in North America as a source of tannin for tanning leather. It can grow very tall and reach a large girth, the British records being 48 m (157 ft) for height and 5 m (17 ft) for girth. Hemlock can grow in deeper shade than most other trees, and foresters find it useful for filling half-shaded gaps in woods until the time is right for removing taller neighbouring trees. Hemlock can also be grown as a dense clipped hedge. Its foliage has no practical value for indoor decoration, as the needles promptly fall.

Hemlock gained its strange name because early settlers in New England thought that the rank smell of its crushed foliage resembled the odour of the European hemlock plant. This is a tall, highly poisonous weed of watersides,

Western hemlock bears thin, delicately patterned grey bark; its bole is buttressed.

bearing large green leaves and big umbels of white flowers on its green, purple-spotted stem. As can be imagined, there is no botanical relationship between the hemlock plant and the hemlock tree.

161

NORWAY SPRUCE

Picea abies PINACEAE

Everybody knows Norway spruce as the Christmas tree, its evergreen foliage serving as a Christian symbol of everlasting life. Its use as a decorative setting for lights, gifts and ornaments was introduced from Germany by Prince Albert in 1844.

Like all spruces, this European species bears its needles singly, set on short pegs. Pull any green needle, and the peg comes too. But once a needle fades, it falls and leaves the peg behind, creating a rough-surfaced twig with knobs. As the branches and trunk develop, the bark keeps this abrasive roughness, harsh to the touch, though it never gets thick. Norway spruce's grey-brown bark always holds a tinge of rusty red – a good key feature.

The timber within has a uniform pale creamy-brown colour, with no apparent distinction of heartwood. The timber trade calls it 'whitewood'. It is not naturally durable, and as it is hard to treat with preservatives people rarely use it in contact with the ground. Moderately strong and easily worked, it is used on a very large scale in house-building, both carpentry and joinery, and packaging work of all kinds; also for telegraph poles, mine props, ladders and ships' masts. It makes good chipboard and first-rate paper pulp.

Expanding shoots of Norway spruce burst from reddish-brown buds in April and open pale-green needles. These darken later and persist for several years. Male flowers, borne in groups in leaf axils of older shoots, are clusters of golden stamens. They scatter yellow, wind-borne pollen in May and then wither away. Crimson female flowers open as bud-like structures near branch tips, and stand upright at first. After pollination they turn purple and enlarge rapidly to become, by autumn, hard brown woody cones that always droop downwards, a good key feature.

Norway spruce cones are long and cylindrical, tapering to a blunt tip. Their smooth triangular scales form elegant spirals. Beneath each scale ripen two tiny seeds, each with a brown papery wing. When the scales open in spring, the seeds drift away on the wind. On sprouting, they open first a tuft of about twenty seed-leaves, and then bear normal foliage.

Norway spruce grows wild on all the high mountain ranges of Europe, and across the northern plains of

Norway spruce has reddish-brown bark with shallow plates; its base becomes buttressed.

Scandinavia and Russia. It was introduced to Britain in about 1500, and has since been planted on most woodland estates as a timber tree. It can reach 42 m (138 ft) tall and 4.3 m (14 ft) round. Its bark can be used for tanning leather, its leaves flavour spruce beer, and pitch was once obtained by tapping its trunk.

SITKA SPRUCE

Picea sitchensis PINACEAE

This distinctive conifer is today more widely planted in the British Isles than any other forest tree, for it gives very high yields of exceptionally useful timber, and tolerates poor soils. You will find it thriving, however, only in the forests of Scotland, Wales, Ireland, the north of England, and Devon or Cornwall. It demands high rain-

Sitka spruce shows an intricate pattern of greyish plates on a chocolate-brown base; buttresses develop at foot.

fall and moist atmospheres for successful growth, and is unhappy under the drier and sunny climates of the Midlands or south and east England. Its homeland is the Pacific coast of North America, from Alaska south to California, and even there it thrives only near the rainy western shore. It takes its name from the small seaport of Sitka, on Baranoff Island in southern Alaska, which was once important as a Russian settlement before the Americans, in 1867, bought that remote country.

Sitka spruce is easily known by its silvery-blue needles;

it is sometimes called 'silver spruce'. Every needle has a sharp point. This makes Sitka spruce unacceptable as a Christmas tree, but helps to protect it from hungry sheep or deer. The pretty cones are very distinctive. Pale brown in colour, they are egg shaped and have papery-textured, crinkly scales. The minute brown seeds, borne in pairs below each scale, have papery brown wings; it takes 150,000 seeds to weigh one pound. Seedlings start life with a whorl of blue-green seed-leaves, and then open typical solitary needles, set on the pegs that characterize all spruces.

Sitka spruce tolerates wind blast, and even salt-laden gales off the wild Atlantic Ocean, better than any other tree, so it makes good shelter-belts. Always erect, it quickly grows tall with a stout trunk. It can reach 50 m (165 ft) with girths up to 7.6 m (25 ft). Its bluish-grey bark has at first the typical spruce roughness, but later becomes smooth, and eventually the surface layers break off in flat, round plates.

The timber of Sitka spruce is very pale, almost white to pale creamy-brown in colour, with no apparent distinction of heartwood. It is rarely used out of doors because it is not naturally durable, nor is it easy to treat with preservatives. Under dry conditions it proves a sound material for building and packaging, having satisfactory strength combined with even texture and good working properties. Its pale colour and regular substance makes it ideal for high-grade chipboard which is widely used today in furniture making. It is the world's best timber for paper pulp, because its fibres are tough, long and white. They change shape during the paper-making process to form flat ribbons which yield a smooth surface, and bond tightly together, giving the paper supple strength.

LARCHES

Larix decidua   PINACEAE
L. *kaempferi*
L. × *eurolepis*

Larches are the only common coniferous trees that shed their needles in winter. This habit is linked to their natural homes on high mountains where the soil is frozen for six months of the year and most evergreen trees would die of drought. They are easily known, at any time of year, by the presence of woody knobs along their twigs, which also carry long grooves on an otherwise smooth surface. Near the tip of each shoot the needles are borne singly, but everywhere else they are set in neat rosettes around the knobs, which are technically 'short shoots' which never grow longer. Larch needles are bright emerald-green when, early in April, they emerge in little tufts from the knobs. They are always soft in texture, unlike the hard needles of evergreen conifers. In October they fade to bright golden, pale orange or russet brown, before falling to leave the twigs leafless through winter.

Male flowers of larch open in clusters on young shoots in late April. Each is a group of stamens that scatter yellow pollen on the winds. Female flowers, often called 'larch roses', are pretty red or white rosettes, often gathered for decoration, which open on young twigs at some distance from the males. After pollination, the female flowers turn green and expand rapidly through the summer. By October they have become hard, woody, barrel-shaped cones, with blunt broad scales and a hollow, not pointed, tip. Next spring their scales slowly open and gradually release oval brown seeds, with triangular papery wings, two from each scale. Each seedling has a whorl of seed-leaves, followed by a shoot that bears solitary needles; needles grouped on knobs do not appear until the second year, or even later.

European larch's fibrous grey-brown bark forms a pattern of long irregular plates.

Larch bark has a fibrous character and becomes thick and soft in relation to that of most other conifers. It is pale greyish brown and its rough surface is broken by a pattern of fissures. The timber below has a pale-cream outer sapwood zone and an inner heartwood coloured reddish brown which is naturally durable; the sapwood is easily treated with preservatives. Larch timber is stronger than most conifers and is used widely for fencing and building repairs. The planking of wooden fishing craft, still built in Scotland, is always home-grown larch. Because of their good timber properties and attractive appearance larches are planted everywhere.

European larch, *Larix decidua*, introduced from the Alps in about 1600, has pale-yellow twigs, pale-green needles and straight cone scales. It can reach 45 m (146 ft) in height and 5.8 m (19 ft) in girth. Japanese larch, *L. kaempferi*, grown here since 1861, has rust-brown twigs, blue-green needles, and reflexed cone scales, and grows

169

Summer

Spring

winter

European

Japanese

faster; it has already reached 37 m (120 ft) tall and 2.7 m (9 ft) in girth. Hybrid larch, L. × *eurolepis*, raised by crossbreeding these two, has intermediate characters, such as mid-brown twigs, truly green needles, and cone scales with only their edges reflexed. It grows faster still, to dimensions approaching those of Japanese larch.

170

SCOTS PINE

Pinus sylvestris PINACEAE

Scots pine is so called because, although it is widespread in Europe and was once native over the whole of the British Isles, it survives in strength as a wild tree in the Highlands of Scotland. It is easily known by its pinkish-grey bark, which develops broad plates as the trunk expands; on younger and higher branches the bark is often bright orange-red and even the grey twigs show russet

171

shades. The distinctive needles, set in pairs, are short, twisted and *bluish* green, another key point. Buds are rust-red and *blunt*.

In April these buds break and a shoot bearing opening pairs of needles, pale green at first, expands rapidly. Lower down the stem, clusters of male flowers open in early May. Each is a group of numerous stamens which scatter clouds of golden pollen on the wind. At the same time the little female flowers open as one or two crimson globes, each smaller than a pea, right at the tip of the newly expanded foliage shoot. After pollination they turn brown and hard but expand only slightly. A whole year later they resume growth, expanding rapidly and changing shape to become soft green cones about 4 cm (1½ in.) long; these are full sized by autumn. The cone scales stay tightly shut until the next spring, that is, two years after the flowers first appeared. Then they become brown and woody, and open gradually.

The seeds, borne in pairs below each scale, have an oval brown kernel and a papery brown wing that aids wind dispersal. After falling on moist soil each seed puts down a root, then raises the seed cap on a pink stalk. The cap falls off to release a tuft of about twenty green seed-leaves. The first shoot that follows bears single needles, like a tuft of grass; paired needles follow in the second year.

Scots pine trees have a strong red-brown resinous heartwood, within a pale-brown sapwood zone. Not naturally durable, but easily treated with preservatives, this timber gives long service as fence posts, telegraph poles and railway sleepers, objects that are always in contact with wet ground. A major commercial timber, it is used throughout Europe for building, packaging, pit props and paper pulp. When marketed in Britain, it carries the trade name of 'redwood'.

Our tallest Scots pine, at Oakley Park in Shropshire, reaches 37 m (120 ft). The stoutest, in Glen Affric Forest,

Scots pine bark, first grey, then pink to orange-brown, matures as pinkish-grey plates, with dark-brown fissures.

Inverness-shire is 7.3 m (24 ft) round. Trees felled at the royal forest of Ballochbuie, on Deeside, have been shown, by actual counts of their annual rings, to exceed 300 years in age.

Native pinewoods survive in about thirty glens, mostly isolated from each other, in the Scottish Highlands. The finest stand in the straths of the River Spey, around Aviemore, and the Dee, near Ballater. Plantations of Scots pine have been made on nearly every large estate and forest throughout Britain, for it proves a reliable tree, though not a fast timber producer. It has become naturalized over many commons in the south of England.

173

CORSICAN PINE

Pinus nigra variety *maritima*   PINACEAE

This stately tree, which originates on the Mediterranean island of Corsica, is nowadays widely planted in the Midlands and south of England, and even locally on the coasts of Wales and eastern Scotland. Wherever it gets ample summer sunshine it thrives and produces timber faster than the commoner Scots pine. It grows vigorously on sand dunes and resists both drought and salty sea winds. It has been used to stabilize sand dunes at Culbin in Morayshire and Newborough in Anglesey.

Corsican pine is easily recognized by its needles, which are set in pairs like those of other common pines, but are much longer, grey-green in colour, and *twisted*. Its distinctive buds are broad at the base, then taper abruptly to a sharp tip. The bark is pale grey, and contrasts with the reddish bark of Scots pine or the black bark of lodgepole pine. Branching is very regular, with annual whorls of side branches set at clear intervals up the trunk. The timber has a wide creamy-brown outer sapwood zone and a central core of mid-brown heartwood. Strong, and easily treated with preservatives if so required, it serves the same purposes as Scots pine.

In May, just as the new shoots are opening pale-green needles, Corsican pine bears conspicuous clusters of large yellow male flowers, which scatter showers of golden pollen. Female flowers, borne at tips of new shoots, are tiny red-brown globes that develop, during their first year, into small brown, round, immature cones. During their second year they expand rapidly and mature through a soft green stage into brown woody cones that are always *oblique*, having the scales on one side larger than those on the other. The cone scales open in spring to release large grey-brown winged seeds. The vigorous seedling has a soft pink stem bearing a whorl of many blue-green seed-leaves.

These are followed by large bluish-green, twisted, solitary needles; typical paired needles first appear in the second spring.

In the mountains of Corsica this pine grows wild in magnificent forests where huge trees stand for 360 years or more. Introduced in 1759, it was first planted as an ornamental tree, and many parks hold fine specimens. The tallest in Britain scales 45 m (147 ft) while the stoutest is 4.6 m (15 ft) round. Thetford Chase, in sunny East Anglia, is England's largest Corsican pine forest.

Allied to the Corsican pine is the Austrian pine, *Pinus*

175

nigra variety *nigra*, which can be distinguished by its *straight* needles. It grows slowly and bears large, rough, irregular branches close together. This means that there are large knots in its wood and therefore timber merchants dislike it. But it has been widely planted as shelterbelts where few other trees thrive, along sea coasts or on exposed hilltops with chalk or limestone soils, and there its close branching proves an advantage.

LODGEPOLE PINE

Pinus contorta P<small>INACEAE</small>

When early explorers crossed the great plains of North America they found that the Indians on the eastern foothills of the Rocky Mountains used the straight stems of a peculiar pine tree to support the skins of their lodges or wigwams, hence the name 'lodgepole pine'. Botanists, finding the same tree on the exposed Pacific coast of Oregon, where its stems were bent by the sea winds,

Lodgepole pine has thin dark-grey bark, broken into small irregular plates.

thought up the Latin name of *Pinus contorta*, meaning twisted pine! Nobody thought much of this tree until, around 1930, Irish foresters found it grew vigorously with them, enjoying a similar climate near a western ocean – this time the Atlantic and thriving on poor exposed hill land. Now it is very widely planted in north and west Scotland, too, and many plantations can be found elsewhere in the British Isles.

At first sight lodgepole pine looks like Scots pine, for it bears needles in pairs and has similar buds. A closer look shows that these needles are dark green, rather than blue-green, and somewhat longer. As the stems grow stouter, the bark ages in quite a different pattern to that of Scots pine. Instead of turning red and forming plates, it becomes black and develops a rough surface broken into small irregular squares. Lodgepole pine cones show a constant key feature, for every scale bears a small sharp prickle on its face. Cones are often borne by quite young trees, no bigger than bushes. The tree's other features, namely, male and female flowers, and seedlings, resemble those of Scots pine.

The land on which lodgepole pine is planted is usually very poor upland grazings or deer forest, with either deep peaty soil or a mineral soil that was compacted thousands of years ago by Ice Age glaciers. Before trees can thrive the peaty soil must be drained, or the hard soil broken up, and the Forestry Commission uses ploughs of varied patterns, drawn by powerful crawler tractors, to prepare the land in this way. As the soil is poor in nutrients, phosphate fertilizers are usually applied in small but critical quantities to give the trees a good start.

Seed for new lodgepole pine plantations is collected from carefully chosen forests in British Columbia, where good trees grow in a climate like that of western Britain. It is sown in nurseries, and the trees are transplanted later to another nursery bed, or else the seedlings are raised in little pots of peaty soil which can be transferred to the ploughed moorlands. There the small trees start their forest life in full exposure to icy gales, frost and snow, but prove so hardy that they soon grow upright stems, and expand vigorous side branches which meet to form flourishing plantations.

The timber of lodgepole pine has pale-brown sapwood and dark-brown heartwood. Reasonably strong, it is used for the same purposes as Scots pine. The tallest British tree measured so far is 28 m (92 ft) high, and the stoutest 3.4 m (11 ft) round.

WESTERN RED CEDAR

Thuja plicata   PINACEAE

This is one of many trees found in various parts of the world which have been called 'cedar' because they bear fragrant foliage or have scented wood, like the Cedar of Lebanon, *Cedrus libani*, mentioned in the Bible. Botanically, the tree described here is quite distinct, and so are most other 'cedars'. It is called 'western' because it grows wild only near the west coast of North America, and 'red' because of its reddish twigs and freshly cut wood. It is the cedar that is widely used in North America and Europe for bungalows, sheds and greenhouses, and also for durable roofing tiles called 'shingles'. Orange-red at first, it mellows to a lovely silvery grey, and lasts indefinitely.

The evergreen foliage of western red cedar is fern-like, with the small leaves clasping the twigs, hiding both twig and buds completely. The leaves are 'solid' to the touch, and you may feel the hidden buds below them; they tend to be yellowish green, and when they fall reveal rust-red twigs. These small points are important, since they distinguish the western red cedar from the similar Lawson cypress. When crushed, the foliage has a rather rank, strong odour. The leading shoot always stands erect, whereas that of Lawson cypress often droops.

Both male and female flowers on the western red cedar are small and bud-like. They open in May, and pollination is by wind. In autumn the curious small cones open. They are pale brown, oval and pointed, and hold two little brown winged seeds beneath each slender scale. Seedlings bear two seed-leaves, and then a short succession of single slender needles – the ancestral pattern of the tree. The normal, twig-clasping pattern of foliage follows.

Western red cedar is widely planted as a hedge shrub, for it makes a dense evergreen barrier and stands clipping well. You may also find it planted in woodlands. Its

Western red cedar grows a buttressed base, clad in red-brown, thin, fibrous bark.

light, strong, naturally durable timber, which has only a narrow pale sapwood zone, has varied uses. It makes safe ladder poles and is a good joinery and constructional timber. The Haida Indians of British Columbia hollowed

out cedar trunks to make their war canoes and build their houses; also, because it lasted longer than all others, they carved it into totem poles to record their tribal histories.

In North America this cedar stands for 800 years and becomes a huge tree, up to 61 m (200 ft) tall and 15 m (50 ft) round. The tallest western red cedar in Britain scales 38 m (125 ft) and also has the stoutest girth at 6 m (19 ft).

LAWSON CYPRESS

Chamaecyparis lawsoniana   PINACEAE

This attractive tree, now widely planted in parks and
gardens, was discovered on the west coast of North
America, in California, by the exploring botanist Andrew
Murray, in the year 1854. The expedition had been
sponsored by Peter Lawson, an Edinburgh nurseryman,
and so the tree was named after him.

183

Lawson cypress can be recognized by its fern-like foliage, built up of many tiny needles that clasp the twigs and hide completely the terminal buds. In the spring you may find its bright pink male flowers, which look like buds, at the twig tips. In April they scatter golden, wind-borne pollen. The little female flowers are also bud-like structures, consisting of bluish-green scales set in an open formation. After pollination they ripen by October to small round, pale, greyish-brown cones. If you examine these you will find that each has about eight odd-looking scales, with central stalks and flat tops. Below each scale, two to five small brown seeds ripen, with a papery wing surrounding each kernel. The seedlings that arise next spring are at first quite unlike their parents. They have two seed-leaves, then thin straight needles set along a stalk. Later, and always by their second year of growth, they change abruptly to the adult foliage pattern.

Lawson cypress can be distinguished from the very similar western red cedar (*Thuja plicata*) by the thin 'feel' of its foliage fronds. These have a more resinous smell, and the cypress twigs show no red colour. On a typical Lawson cypress, though not on some varieties, the leading shoot droops gracefully downwards.

Lawson cypress bark is thin and dark purplish grey. The sapwood is pale cream in colour and the heartwood purplish brown. The timber is strong, but foresters rarely plant Lawson cypress for timber because its trunk nearly always forks, to give two or three upright stems. This fault makes it unprofitable to saw up the logs. Seldom a big tree, Lawson cypress may grow 37 m (120 ft) tall, and 4 m (13 ft) round.

Gardeners and landscapists find Lawson cypress a very useful tree. It is hardy, evergreen, has no serious pests or diseases, and clothes itself with neat foliage which needs no pruning. Many varieties have been discovered, and these are increased by cuttings. You can choose trees with blue, yellow, silver, or variegated foliage, some very

Lawson cypress has grey-brown bark in thin shaggy plates, and a spreading base.

pretty, others just quaint. Some grow tall and slender, others stay squat, while others again droop or display strange twisted foliage patterns.

JUNIPER

Juniperus communis   PINACEAE

This remarkable evergreen conifer may be mistaken at
first sight for a gorse bush, though some individuals
develop a tree-like form and grow up to 9 m (30 ft) tall.
Once you crush a few spiky needles, their sharp resinous
scent will reveal its true identity. Close inspection shows
that these needles are grouped in threes, though each is
separate, and that they bear on their upper surface a
silvery band of wax that restricts water loss. The buds
are very small and brown.

In spring juniper bears clusters of yellow male flowers
amid its needles. The female flowers which receive their
wind-borne pollen are little green globes, likewise hidden
in the foliage. During the summer they enlarge to become
juicy berries, which turn purplish black by the autumn
of the following year, eighteen months after pollination.
Each berry is really a modified cone, made up of about
eight scales, each with a central stalk. They attract birds

Juniper grows several spreading stems, clad in thin, fragrant, pinkish-grey bark.

which help to scatter the small hard seeds hidden in their pulp. These seeds lie dormant in the soil throughout the following year. Then they sprout, in spring, and bear two seed-leaves followed by the characteristic foliage.

Juniper was once widespread on waste lands in most parts of the British Isles but today it is only common in the Scottish Highlands. Elsewhere you may find it locally in Galloway, the north of England, the chalky Chiltern Hills, the downs of the south-east, and more plentifully on the Wiltshire chalk around Salisbury. Its decline is due to the burning of pastures, since it is very inflammable, or to smothering by faster-growing broadleaved trees where sheep-grazing has ceased. Cottagers also cut it to make kindling for their household fires.

187

Juniper berries can be distilled to yield a fragrant strongly flavoured oil called oil of juniper. This is used in perfumery and exotic cookery, and was formerly applied in medicine. Its widest use, however, is to flavour grain spirits to make gin, a drink that draws its name from the French word for juniper, *genévrier*.

Juniper has a flaky, fibrous, grey bark. Its thin woody stems have white sapwood and pinkish-brown heartwood, and are fragrant throughout. Owing to its small size, juniper wood is only used for small decorative carving and inlay, for example, as handles for forks or Highlander's dirks.

INDEX

Numbers in italics indicate pages on which the principal illustrations of each tree appear

189

SEEDLING TREES

Lime
Tilia × vulgaris

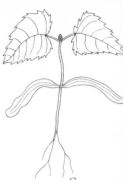

Sycamore
Acer pseudoplatanus

Cherry
Prunus avium

Ash
Fraxinus excelsior